CW00517401

An Introduction to
EXISTENTIALISM, PHENOMENOLOGY,
and HERMENEUTICS

An Introduction to
EXISTENTIALISM, PHENOMENOLOGY,
and HERMENEUTICS

Anselm K. Jimoh

Ebony Books

Published by
Ebony Books & Kreations
3, Gbolasere Street, Ologuneru
Ibadan, Oyo State
0802 208 2826, 0705 936 5446, 0705 936 5447
E-mail: ebonykreations74@yahoo.com

© Anselm K. Jimoh
jimohanselm1@yahoo.com

All Rights Reserved

ISBN 979-887-332-852-9

Published, March 2014

Dedication

To Rev. Fr. David Nolan
(A very good man)

Acknowledgements

This short introduction to Existentialism, Phenomenology, and Hermeneutics is a result of my discussion with Year Four (400 level) seminarians of SS. Peter and Paul Seminary, Bodija, Ibadan (2012/2013 Academic session). I am, therefore, grateful to all of them in that class for their participation in the discussion. They prompted my interest in preparing a handbook to guide students who will be taking the course in subsequent years.

I appreciate all who contributed academically to this project, especially Prof. Chris E. Ukhun, Dr. Remi Aiyede, Rev. Fr. Anthony Ewherido, Ph.D, and Rev. Fr. Anselm Ekhelar, Ph.D. Thanks for your useful pieces of advice, corrections, and written contributions, to this text.

I am very grateful to Rev. Fr. David Nolan of the Archdiocese of New York. He provided me with the conducive atmosphere, to further research into the topics in this short study guide, for students in philosophy and the general reader.

I thank my friends; Rev. Frs. Ezekiel Owoye, Yakubu-Gowon Salami, John Odeyemi, Joseph Iyamah, Lawrence Adorolo, Francis Ikhianosimhe, and Polycarp Imoagene, as well as Mr. Polycarp Oboro for their reliable friendship and constant encouragement. I will not forget Nwodo Naset Obiora, who once again, proved very reliable with his secretariat assistance.

Finally, I thank all those who supported me financially to ensure this publication sees the light of day. I am really grateful to you all.

Preface

Philosophy prides itself as an expression of man's rational abilities in its most racy elements. Philosophizing is an expression of man's freedom of thought in its encumbered manner. Philosophy does not aim to master a body of facts; rather it seeks to enable students to think clearly and sharply through a set of facts. Indeed, training in philosophy is defined by the logical and critical thinking skills it imparts. A typical object of any philosophical training will include the need to make students able to critically analyze and assess arguments, discover hidden assumptions, construct logically tight arguments and express ideas clearly and precisely in both speech and writing.

Yet every student of philosophy is exposed to the history of thought, including a variety of schools of thought in philosophy. Given the tendency to bias in human reasoning owing largely to previous experiences, which, to a large extent, condition the thinking, orientation, dispositions, attitudes, tendencies and world views of individuals, would it not be a good ideas if students are merely exposed to the rudiments of logic and methods of philosophical inquiry and allowed to proceed from there on their own? Why expose them to various philosophical ideas that may affect their world view and orientation? The answer is that it is precisely by exploring and understanding the history of thought and the various schools of thought that the methods of philosophical inquiry are illustrated and seen at work. Indeed, the exposure to the history of thought and thought orientations of great thinkers enables us to appreciate our human patrimony and challenges us to render our own contribution to the intellectual legacies of the human race.

This book provides an impressive discussion of Existentialism, Phenomenology, and Hermeneutics – schools of philosophy that reflect the direction of philosophy in the first part of the twentieth century, a period characterized by monumental changes in politics, economy, and society – defined by two world wars and the great

7

depression such the world is yet to witness again. The schools of thought express man's predicament in the world and how he has engaged the experience of this predicament in those gruesome historical moments. They represent not only how man applied his reason to make sense of the world in the context of the great events of the period, but also man's reflection on the methods and modes of thought with which we comprehend the world of which our thought and consciousness are a part of.

Existentialism, Phenomenology, and Hermeneutics are linked together by the notion of grounding, reflexivity, and humanization. Existentialists maintain that human beings are not merely "rational animals with language, they are also feeling, emoting, intuiting beings – who create and recreate our world through free choices." There are a variety of ways to apprehend our world, phenomenology offers a "practice or method" of interpreting "lived experience" through vivid and detailed descriptions; to expose, uncover, or reveal "universal" elements of human existence that structure our practical, "particular" empirical situations. Similarly, hermeneutics is the practice of interpretation to clarify and deepen our understanding of things that we engage.

The book explores each of these schools of thought in three ways. In the first instance, it clarifies the flagship concept of each of the schools of thought, exploring their usage and analyzing their meaning. Sometimes, it goes on to state instances of their misuse and misrepresentations. Second, it describes the context and evolution of the ideas of these schools. Third, it discusses the main issues and themes addressed by philosophers associated with each school. This book is a very concise account of the substantive issues addressed by the philosophical schools of existentialism, phenomenology, and hermeneutics, representing a specific movement with its currents of though in philosophy. In engaging these schools, one encounters the challenging uncertainties that surround the methods employed in the philosophical enterprise.

These currents of thought seek to bring down philosophy from its Olympian height of rational speculation above the mundane preoccupation of everyday life into a tool for engaging the challenges of human existence with its frustrations and delights, excitement and sobriety, failures and triumphs, hope and despair, dread and confidence, support and forlornness, pleasures and pain, responsibility and innocence, nativity and mortality. In doing this, new meanings are invested in old concepts and reality is grasped in innovative ways, in its integrated character, in a form different from the dualism that hitherto dominated Western philosophy and from which it is yet to completely free itself.

These schools of thought together represent a movement in the history of philosophy that engages issues that are related to the human predicament. The features of this predicament have intensified in our contemporary society, a society that has been described as a 'risk society', by the revolution in information and communication technology that has enabled the transmission and spread of both beneficial and harmful occurrences across the globe with exceptional speed and impact. Engaging existentialism, phenomenology, and hermeneutics is not just an interesting exercise for students of philosophy seeking to meet the requirements of their degree, it is an effective thought stimulant in the challenge to "think out of the box" in engaging the issues of our times.

Emmanuel Remi Aiyede, Ph.D
Department of Political Science
University of Ibadan

Foreword

Tempted by compelling existential phenomena or issues to decline the invitation to write the Foreword to this book, I was, however, moved by professional imperative, a true sense of duty I owe my former doctoral student, promising and brilliant scholar, and the need to salute the author's courage to re-vibrate essential areas of philosophy, writing this Foreword became an imperative.

I discern that the choice to embark on this timely project was influenced by many considerations. First of these considerations was the desire to find a text of high quality to add to the scanty literature on Existentialism, Phenomenology, and Hermeneutics. Appeal and suitability for the professional philosophers, general readers, and students, in terms of content, style, and presentation, was another consideration.

Many are left with the impression that the *loci* on which the prestige and value of philosophy could be found are, Epistemology, Metaphysics, Ethics, Logic, etc. which are often termed the core areas of philosophy with Existentialism, Phenomenology, Hermeneutics, and with some other branches of philosophy in exclusion. This prestige and value appropriation to the so called core areas of philosophy has an entrenched legacy that has turned our attention away from the life-infusing branches or philosophy such as Existentialism, Phenomenology, and Hermeneutics; they are the Philosophy of life, the fundamental ingredients, which constantly interrogate and resonate the essence of life; they reveal the strength and weakness of man in an intriguing world he had no hand in designing, but in which he must find self-expression and worth. Through this book, the author re-echoes the importance of Being, which the early Greek philosophers were determined to popularize. The profound assertion of Protagoras that "man is the measure of all things" remains eternally true. For Socrates, a 'man must know himself'. Certainly, for Socrates, if this were not so, 'man would be dragged about like a slave'. Martin Heidegger's sentiments in alignment with the Greek reverence for Man or Being articulates that it should be the serious business of philosophy or the critical thinker to bring alive the cardinal question of what it is to be what you are or what is Being?

For many philosophers, as with Anselm Jimoh, there is a 'burgeoning awareness of the importance of autonomy in human value', which he clearly laid out in the parts and chapters in this book.

Admittedly, this book is divided into three parts with each part having its distinctive chapters, introduction, and topics, which are well linked. Part One, which focuses on Existentialism, has three chapters. Chapter One contains the issues of What is Existentialism? Short Historical Account of the Development of Existentialism. These topics form the background or foundation for the reading and comprehension of the themes and characters discussed in Chapters Two and Three.

Chapter Two centres on Existence Precedes Essence, Man, Man and the World, Man and Others, Freedom, Choice, and Responsibility, Facticity, Anguish, and Death. These issues amongst others are pungent and critical. They give coloration to Existentialism.

Key Existentialist Thinkers occupy the whole of Chapter Three. In this regard, Soren Kiekegaard, Friedrich Nietzsche, Martin Heidegger, Jean-Paul Sartre, and Albert Camus are presented and discussed with sensible and clinical audacity; bearing in mind that these characters are the hallmarks of Existentialism.

Part Two is devoted to Phenomenology. Within this part, three chapters form the headlines. Naturally, 'What is Phenomenology?' takes the front burner in terms of providing the basis or articulation of the relevant topics such as the Concept of Phenomenology, Some Definitions of Phenomenology, and the Goals of Phenomenology, which are embedded in the first chapter of this part as Chapter Four of this book.

Chapter Five highlights Husserlian Phenomenology. It deals with the Background to Husserlian Phenomenology, Husserl and the Method of Phenomenology, touching on the issues of Descriptive and Transcendental Phenomenology, The Phenomenological Method, which includes treatment of The Natural Attitude and The Phenomenological Attitude.

In Chapter Six, Key Themes in Phenomenology are carefully deposited. We have here, the question of *Epoche,* The Phenomenological Reduction, The Eidetic Reduction, The Transcendental Reduction, Intentionality, and A Critical Review of Phenomenology.

The last part of this book is on Hermeneutics. It harbors, as it were, The Concept and Development of Hermeneutics, Hermeneutics in Modern and Contemporary Times. Here, characters like Friedrich Schleiermarcher, Wilhelm Dilthey, Martin Heidegger, Hans-Georg Gadamer, and Jurgen Habermas, were discussed.

This illuminating book ends with a conclusion, which summarizes Existentialism, Phenomenology, and Hermeneutics. Of course, an extensive bibliography to guide the reader in a further research and an index, for easy location of important themes and names, are also part of this judicious work.

There is no doubt that this text is a colossal effort which reveals the humility, tenacity, and intellectual stature of the author who is determined to prompt and inspire even the docile academics and the general readers for self-awareness and the advancement of humanity. This is a remarkable book that must not remain unnoticed because of its lucidity, contents, and value. The professional philosophers, students, and the general readers will find this book a luscious one.

Christopher E. Ukhun, Ph.D
Professor of Philosophy and Dean
Faculty of Arts, Ambrose Alli University
Ekpoma, Nigeria.

Contents

PART ONE: EXISTENTIALISM

PART ONE: HERMENEUTICS

Introduction

Even in contemporary times, not a few still regard philosophy as a bewildering discipline. So very few students freely choose the discipline or accept courses of this discipline. However, philosophy, by nature and orientation, is a natural result of man's exercise of his rational faculty. Thus, down the ages, and in various forms and contexts, philosophizing has marked the human's exercise of its rational faculty in the effort to resolve perplexing problems of life and living.

The formal beginning of this enterprise in the West is usually traced to the early Greek scholars of the 5th and 6th centuries B.C. who contended with the problem of being and existence. Men of the medieval times faced the issues of God and His existence, while those of the modern era battled with issues of how we come to know what we know and the certainty of such knowledge. Contemporary times have continued with the quest for greater certainty in knowledge of the world outside of us and the status of that world in relation to the knowing consciousness in themes discussed in existentialism, phenomenology, and hermeneutics.

This book, *An Introduction to Existentialism, Phenomenology, and Hermeneutics*, is not only an attempt to carry on the philosophical enterprise, but also a help for students of philosophy towards a full understanding of certain important themes and concepts in contemporary philosophy.

It takes into perspective the themes: Existentialism, Phenomenology, and Hermeneutics. It subjects each to a close conceptual and historical analysis, and in the process establishes what each stands for and the specific goal it pursues. Treatment of each theme is complemented with a discourse of the views of some notable philosophers on the theme.

In this way, the text is presented in seven chapters, three parts, with each part dealing with a particular theme. Part one, consisting of three chapters, focuses on Existentialism and devotes Chapter 1 to providing an answer to the question: What is Existentialism? This prepared the grounds for Themes in Existentialism and Key Existentialist Thinkers that are treated in Chapters 2 and 3 respectively. Part Two of the text turns to Phenomenology with Chapter 4 focusing on what is Phenomenology? While Chapters 5 and 6 deal with Husserlian Phenomenology and Key Themes in Phenomenology respectively.

The final part, Part Three, takes on Hermeneutics and devotes Chapter 7 to an examination of Philosophical Hermeneutics. It examines the concept and its historical development while paying attention to its usage in both modern and contemporary times. It then goes on to take into perspective thoughts of philosophers like Schleiermarcher, Dilthey, Heidegger, Gadamer, and Herbarmas.

The entire text is eventually wrapped up in a General Conclusion in a synthesis of the three main themes treated – Existentialism, Phenomenology, and Hermeneutics.

With this, Fr. Anselm Jimoh has offered a detailed and very easy-to-read exploration of the mentioned themes in a manner that makes each subject matter easily understandable. The student of philosophy and anyone who would like to make sense out of the seeming complexity of the treated themes will, therefore, find in this text a very useful tool.

Rev. Fr. Anselm Ekhelar Ph.D
Department of Philosophy
Seminary of All Saints, Ekpoma

PART ONE

EXISTENTIALISM

Chapter

1

What Is Existentialism?

Introduction

> I do not like to talk about existentialism. It is the nature of an intellectual quest to be undefined. To name it and to define it is to wrap it up and tie the knot. What is left? A finished, already outdated mode of culture, something like a brand of soap – in other words, an idea.
>
> – Jean-Paul Sartre[1]

Sartre's view about defining the notion or concept of existentialism already indicates the problematic associated with attempting to answer the question, "What is existentialism?" It makes better sense for the student studying existentialism to proceed by analyzing the notion of existentialism, understanding its central teachings, especially in the context of their historical background and development, than to begin by trying to define existentialism. According to Richard Appignanesi, existentialism is a seductive word that gives the impression it wants to shed light on human existence but does not deliver positively on this impression.[2] In other words, we cannot, from the content of the teachings of existentialism, construe

---

[1] . J. P. Sartre, (1968), *Search for a Method*, trans. by Harzel E. Barnes, New York: Vintage Books, p.xxxiii.
[2] . R. Appignanesi, (2006), *What do Existentialists Believe?* London: Granta Books, p. 1.

a definition that adequately characterises the concept. This is because existentialists are generally not partners in a unified school of belief as they do not speak with a single consenting voice.[3]

We may refer to existentialism as a "loose title for various philosophies that emphasize certain common themes: the individual, the experience of choice, and the absence of rational understanding of the universe with a consequent dread or sense of absurdity in human life."[4] This claim of Blackburn further consolidates the claims of Sartre and Appignanesi above that existentialism is not an easily definable concept because of the varied views of those referred to as existentialists. These are the thinkers whose views on the question of human existence share one common goal, namely, to awaken our realization of being-in-the-world. Thus, it is the common goal that brings their various views under the collective term; existentialism. It is not a school of thought but rather a movement in the history of modern Western philosophy that has greatly influenced philosophy.

To answer the question, "What is existentialism?" we shall try to understand the historical origin and development of the notion. It will be important to consider the underlying common goal of existentialists and how they fall within the concept of existentialism. This, precisely, is the objective of this introductory chapter.

What is Existentialism?

Existentialism is a philosophical movement that is traced back to Soren Kierkegaard, a Danish 19th Century philosopher, who was the first to stress and articulate the general themes of existentialism. Kierkegaard's work, is therefore, regarded as the origin of existentialism. It is important to note from the outset that, unlike most movements in history that are associated with a leader, for instance, Christianity is identified with the followers of Christ, and Marxism associated with the followers of Karl Marx, existentialism does not have a figurehead or idea to which it is associated. The only common thing among the so-called existentialists is the common situation of existence.

---

[3]. Ibid.
[4]. S. Blackburn, (1996), *Oxford Dictionary of Philosophy*, Oxford: Oxford University Press, p. 129.

Although the term, existentialism was coined by Jean-Paul Sartre, the expression, 'existence philosophy' had, prior to Sartre, been used by Karl Jaspers. In the view of David Cooper, Martin Heidegger and Karl Jaspers had put the word 'existence' to use as we use the word existentialism now, in their works. Both of them had taken the special notion of 'existence' from Kierkegaard, and according to Jaspers, Kierkegaard provides the historical binding meaning of the word.[5] The special use of 'existence' from which the concept of 'existentialism' evolved is the idea of existence referring solely to human beings. This is the idea of the human being as distinct from the being of every other thing. Every other thing that exists is conceived as mere physical object, while the human being is conceived as a being-inexistence. In other words, mere physical objects are not considered as constituent of human existence. The idea that existence highlights here is that human existence, beyond mere physical being, has concern for itself. According to Kierkegaard, the individual is "infinitely interested in existing" and not just existing.[6] What Kierkegaard means by this, is that the individual is able to reflect on his own existence, make decisions about his own existence, and mould his existence in accordance with his reflection. This view of Kierkegaard is in concurrence with that of Heidegger who opines that human beings question their being and make it an issue for themselves.[7] As both philosophers opine, the human being is in the process of always becoming and 'ahead of himself'. These characteristics define existence in its special sense with only reference to the human being and distinguish the human being from mere physical objects that just are. This is the notion that underlines the existentialist notion of "existence precedes essence" which we shall discuss in chapter two below.

There is no doubt that with such characterization as cited above in relation to the special notion of existence as employed by

---

[5] . D. E. Cooper, (1990), *Existentialism*, Oxford UK & Cambridge USA: Blackwell Publishers, p. 2.
[6] . S. Kierkegaard,[A] (1974), *Concluding Unscientific Postscript*, USA: Princeton University Press, p. 268.
[7] . M. Heidegger, (1962), *Being and Time*, Oxford: Blackwell Publishers, p.42H ('H' is a reference to the German original text *Sein und Zeit* provided in the margins of the English translation).

Kierkegaard, which has informed the evolution of the concept of existentialism, we need to elucidate on existence further. This further elucidation is precisely what existentialism is about. Therefore, existentialism as a movement, tries to unravel the implications of our existence in relation to the world, our relationship to each other, and indeed, to the self. These constitute some of the primary themes of existentialism that we shall discuss in chapter two. Generally, existence is conceived by existentialist as "a constant striving, a perpetual choice; it is marked by a radical freedom and responsibility; and it is always prey to a sense of *Angst* which reveals that, for the most part, it is lived inauthentically and in bad faith."[8]

Apart from the fact that Kierkegaard employed the term existence in the special sense in which it has come to be associated with existentialism, and that thinkers after him, who shared his view, adopted it as such, it is noteworthy that Kierkegaard himself did not apply the term arbitrary. A loose tradition prior to Kierkegaard holds that for a certain thing to exist, it must contain certain essences or universals that are instantiated in it. Take for instance, the number 2 exists because it is the particular between the number 1 and 3 and as such, the appropriate essence between 1 and 3. In contrast, the greatest number does not exist, as it is not instantiatable. This implies that the human beings in their existence are peculiarly particular and know themselves immediately without reference to any intermediary.

A more decisive reason for the special use of existence to apply to human beings alone is found in Heidegger and in the origin of the word "exist", which is traceable to Greek and Latin. Heidegger would sometimes use the word with a hyphen, for instance, 'ex-ist', which means 'to stand out from.' In this application and sense, existence expresses the fact that the human being is already beyond or ahead of that which characterizes him at any given time; he stands out from his present 'in' the future towards which he moves.

As a philosophy, existentialism emphasizes human existence as a revolt against the systems of thought that characterized the early part of the 19th Century. According to Macquarrie:

---

[8] . D. E. Cooper, p. 3.

The movement is not a school of philosophy but rather it should be seen as a style of philosophizing. They do not believe in abstract speculation but rather they are interested in concrete human existence. Their philosophizing begins from man rather than from nature.[9]

It evolved as a reactionary trend to the abstract discussions about nature and human knowledge that occupied philosophical discourses at the closing end of modern Western philosophy. It stresses and emphasizes existence as taking precedence over essence. By 'existence' we mean that which is in being; it is the main subject matter of metaphysics, especially ontology. Most philosophers who are concerned with existence, generally are in fact, preoccupied exclusively with human existence, and that is the sense in which it is used in this text. On the other hand, 'essence' refers to the basic or primary element in the being of a thing. This is the nature of the thing, without which, it cannot be what it is. The phrase, 'existence precedes essence' implies that human existence is prior to his essence; meaning that, we exist first before we become whatever we want to become. Sartre stresses this point saying:

It means, first of all, that man exist, turns up, appears on the scene, and only afterwards defines himself. If man as the existentialist sees him, is indefinable, it is because at first, he is nothing. Only afterwards will he be something and he himself will have made what he will be.[10]

As a philosophical movement, existentialism is against all objectives and abstraction. It takes human existence as the point of departure for philosophy. Human existence, for the existentialists, encompasses the totality of the individual such that what the individual does and feels, his basic inclinations, associations, etc. are all part and parcel of his existence.

---

[9] . J. Macquarrie, (1983), *Existentialism*, New York: World Publishing Company, p. 14.
[10] . J. P. Sartre, (1947), *Existentialism*, trans. by Bernard Reidman, New York: Philosophical Library, p. 18.

Existentialism stands out as the most influential philosophical movement in contemporary Western philosophy. It is definitely not a homogenous school, nor is it a coherent system of philosophy, since the existentialists, that is, those who are associated with this movement, differ widely from one another and they all had their individual emphasis and did not belong to the same movements in society. For instance, Kierkegaard was a devout Christian; Nietzsche was an atheist; Sartre was a Maxist, and Heidegger was briefly a Nazi. While Sartre insisted on the freedom of the will, Nietzsche denied it, and Heidegger would hardly mention it. These are thinkers with "certain common ancestry, common interests and common presuppositions sustained by a commitment to improve the lot of man in this miserable world."[11]This, however, does not eliminate the fundamental fact that existentialism represents a certain attitude in which the existentialists share a common concern for the individual and for personal responsibility. Existentialism is, therefore, suspicious of, and in fact, hostile to, the submersion of the individual in larger groups or forces. [12] It comes as a philosophical tradition that vigorously questions and challenges the philosophical culture of the pre-20th Century era; it accuses philosophy of being overly abstract and speculative and of relying too much on logical systems. According to Paul Roubiczek,

> Existentialism is a rejection of all purely abstract thinking, of a purely logical or scientific philosophy: in short, a rejection of the absoluteness of reason. Instead, it insists that philosophy should be connected with the historical situation in which it find itself and that it should be, not interested in abstract speculation; but a way of life. It should be a philosophy capable of being lived.[13]

---

[11] . W. Olajide, (2000), "Existentialism" in K. A. Owolabi (ed.), *Issues and Problems in Philosophy*, Ibadan: GROVACS (NETWORK), p. 128.

[12] . R. Solomon, (2000), "existentialism" in T. Mautner, (ed.), *The Penguin Dictionary of Philosophy*, London: Penguin Books, p. 187.

[13] P. Roubiczek, (1964), *Existentialism: For and Against*, Cambridge: University Press, p. 10.

Existentialist philosophers belong to the same movement within the context of the fact that they make human existence the central point of philosophy. They are together opposed to rational philosophy. They see philosophy as having the more positive role to play in analyzing the human person in his existential situation. This implies that philosophy should consider the factors and forces that assail the human person as its primary subject-matter, rather than the abstract discussions of the analytic movements of modern Western philosophy, which has ascribed very little to this area of paramount concern. As David Nyong puts it, "philosophy for the existentialists must be brought down from the high heavens where abstract speculations have placed it."[14] This implies that philosophy must not be separated from man as the speculator; man must be the matrix on which philosophizing revolves. For existentialism, if philosophy must be serious investigation into truth and reality, it must focus on the existence of the human being.

Therefore, existentialism is against rationalism on the basis that rationalism emphasizes only the intellect in the understanding of reality. It is also against realism on the basis that realism talks about reality as that which is 'given' far away from the reality of the human being who perceives it. Existentialism is also against the situation of humans in the industrial society; situations in which humans are dehumanized and depersonalized and therefore treated like a machine. It contends that the industrialized society does not accord humans their humanity and the dignity due to them as the inventor of machine. For existentialism, the human being must be given his/her due place, so it emphasizes the primacy of the existing individual.

What Existentialism is not

While we can confidently assert that existentialism is what everyone may have heard of, we have to immediately assert that existentialism has a popular image that is full of misconception. By this, I mean that there are many conceptions of existentialism that do not truly represent the notion that it stands for. The misconceptions of

---

[14] D. Nyong, (1996), *Rudiments of Philosophy and Logic*, Lagos: Obaroh and Ogbinaka Publishers Limited, p. 40.

existentialism are traced to popular histories and ideas, dictionary
definitions, and encyclopedia summaries of the notion of
existentialism.

For instance, *The Oxford Companion to French Literature* (1st ed.),
describes existentialism as "the metaphysical expression of the
spiritual dishevelment of a post-war age." J. M. Roberts, a European
historian, describes existentialism as "the assertion that life is more
than logic ... that the subjective and personal must be more highly
valued and the objective and intellectualized must be depreciated."[15]
The 5th edition of *The Concise Oxford English Dictionary* describes
existentialism as "An anti-intellectual philosophy of life, holding that
man is free and responsible, based on the assumption that reality as
existence can only be lived, but can never become the object of
thought."

The above descriptions of existentialism summarize the
misconceptions of the notion and concept of existentialism; the last
one is particularly vexing. Cooper summarizes the various
misconceptions of existentialism as a popular view which can be
expressed thus:

> Existentialism was a philosophy born out of the *Angst* of post-
> war Europe, out of a loss of faith in the ideals of progress,
> reason and science which had led to Dresden and Auschwitz.
> If not only God, but reason and objective value are dead, then
> man is abandoned in an absurd and alien world. The
> philosophy for man in this "age of distress" must be a
> subjective, personal one. A person's remaining hope is to
> return to his "inner self", and live in whatever ways he feels
> are true to that self. The hero for this age, the existentialist
> hero, lives totally free from the constraints of discredited
> traditions, and commits himself unreservedly to the demands
> of his inner, authentic being.[16]

Cooper's summary of the misconceptions of existentialism aptly
tells the tale of good intentions going wrong. These misconceptions,
according to him are the resultant consequences of misinterpretations
of the fictional works of Simone de Beauvoir, titled the *Tabou* and the

---

[15]. J. M. Roberts, (1977), *Europe 1880-1945*, London: Longman, p. 467.
[16] D. E. Cooper, pp. 11-12.

Pergola, and the late 1940s movie on the young Juliette Greco, as well as the outright distortions of Sartre's *Being and Nothingness*, where Sartre's idea of existential freedom is taken as license to behave as unconventionally as possible. Over reliance on some existentialists' fictional novels, like Albert Camus' *The Outsider*, and Sartre's hurriedly written lecture on *Existentialism and Humanism*, which was later published to his regrets when he found out passages that encouraged the notion that commitment and moral decision can only be irrational, also contributed to the misconceptions under discussion.

Agreed that existentialism is a post-war movement inspired by the human conditions of the time, it is certainly not a post-war dishevelment, despair, or malaise. To conceive existentialism as such is to mix up existentialism as a philosophy and existentialism as a vogue. If we describe existentialism as an expression of an age, we suggest that the claims of existentialism are temporary and valid only locally to the places gravely affected by the destructions of the Second World War and not to the whole of humanity. This already negates the universality of the distinctiveness of human existence, the interdependence of mind and world, our existential freedom, etc. It means these phenomena do not apply to all peoples, at all times, and in all places. This is definitely not the case, as the distinctiveness of human existence, the interdependence of mind and world, human existential freedom, and other existential characteristics of the human being are true of all human beings, at all times, and in all places. More so, they are perennial conditions of human beings that are not restricted to particular situations in particular places in the history of humankind.

Existentialism is wrongly described as a metaphysical expression of post-war dishevelment, despair, and malaise because it supports the notion that *Angst* and despair are, in a particular way, symptoms of the 20th century condition. There is no debating the fact that most thinkers, whose writings are considered existentialist, speak a lot about these notions, but we must understand their use of these notions properly and not misconstrue them. Kierkegaard, for instance, used "despair" to describe the position of somebody whose life hinges upon a condition outside of itself;[17] rather than a mood of hopeless gloom, as it is generally thought. Sartre uses it to describe a situation where "there is no God and no prevenient design, which can adapt the world ... to my will."[18] Against common opinion that existentialists use *Angst* to refer to the fear in our minds when faced with the reality of a dangerous, uncertain world, existentialists actually use the term to describe "a sense of freedom, of a capacity to strike out on one's own in the formation of a scheme of beliefs and values."[19]

Existentialism is not an anti-intellectualist philosophy. This erroneous view comes from the fact that the existentialist argues his position by closely describing everyday life, pointing out our understanding of ourselves, and exposing the lack of coherence in rival positions. The existentialist is not esoteric in his investigation and claims. While the existentialist is not an irrationalist, he is certainly not a rationalist in the sense that we contrast the rationalist with the empiricist. By this, I mean that the existentialist does not subscribe to innate ideas. This is not because he subscribes to the empiricist view either, that knowledge is a product of experience. The existentialist rather relates with the existential situation of our being, dealing with the forces and conditions that surround our existence. Existentialism emphasizes the humanness of the world. The emphasis of the existentialist on the humanness of the world has also given rise to the misconception that existentialism denies the objectivity of the world and therefore, suggests that existentialism is a subjectivist philosophy. It is true that existentialism pays particular attention to the individual or subject; that, however, does not make it a subjectivist philosophy.

---

[17] . S. Kierkegaard,[B] (1974). *Either/Or*, vol. 2, Princeton: Princeton University Press, p. 240.
[18] . J. P. Sartre, (1966), *Existentialism and Humanism*, New York: Methuen and Company Ltd., p. 39.
[19] . D. E. Cooper, pp. 13-14.

Some Definitions of Existentialism

We cannot easily define existentialism since it includes a variety of attitudes, views and opinions. The *Webster's New World Dictionary* defines it as:

> The doctrine that existence takes precedence over essence and holding that man is totally free and responsible for his acts. The responsibility is the source of dread and anguish that encompass mankind.

In like manner, the *American Heritage Dictionary of English Language* defines it as, "a philosophy that emphasizes the uniqueness and isolation of the individual experience in a hostile indifferent universe, regards human existence as unexplainable and stresses freedom of choice and responsibility for the consequences of one's acts." According to Nwachukwu, the above definitions contrast with the behaviorist view that humans live under the control of their environment, governed by laws.[20]

The *Internet Encyclopedia of Philosophy* describes existentialism as "a catch-all term for those philosophers who consider the nature of the human condition as a key philosophical problem and who share the view that this problem is best addressed through ontology."[21] It is a "philosophical movement that stresses the importance of personal experience and responsibility and the demands they make on the individual, who is seen as a free agent in a deterministic and seemingly meaningless universe."[22] These two definitions highlight the following points about existentialism:

i.   That man forms his essence in the course of his life resulting from his personal choices.

---

[20] . A. Nwachukwu, (1994), "Existentialist Themes in African Novel" in *Ufahamu:*
Journal of African Activist Association, vol.xiv, no.1.
[21] . "Existentialism" in the *Internet Encyclopedia of Philosophy*, www.iep.utm.edu/existent/ (Retrieved on 19/3/13).
[22] . "Existentialism" in www.thefreedictionary.com/existentialism (Retrieved on 19/3/13).

ii.   That man creates his own nature through his personal
freedom, decisions and commitment.

According to Blessing Agidigbi, "existentialism can be defined as
a philosophy of subjectivity or selfhood."[23] This definition brings out
the individuality of the subject matter, which is man and his
conditions of existence. It should not be misconceived as suggesting
that existentialism is a subjectivist philosophy, rather, it points to the
fact that man is seen as an isolated individual existing in an indifferent
or hostile universe, yet responsible for his actions as he makes free
choices that shape his destiny. It is within this context that we
understand Joseph Omoregbe's definition of existentialism as "the
philosophy of human existence, a philosophy preoccupied with what
it means for a human being to exist."[24] This definition highlights the
fact that existentialists are concerned, not with inanimate objects that
are, like stones and trees, or even lower animals, but with human
existence. The important point here, as noted above, is the fact that
the word 'existence' is not used in existentialism in its classical
meaning as referring to all that is being, but specifically, it refers to
the human mode of existence or being. For the existentialists, only
human beings exist, other beings are. They simply are but not exist.
Existence, for the existentialist, therefore means, "to be personally
committed to a freely chosen way of life; it means being conscious of
the problems of human life with all the choices open to man and
opting for a certain way of life while assuming responsibility for it."[25]
In this sense or meaning of existence, it is only humans that we can
say exist. Heidegger points this out lucidly when he asserts:

The being that exits is man. Man alone exists. Trees are but
they do not exist. Angels are but they do not exist...[26]

[23]. B. Agidigbi, (2006), *Issues and Themes in Existentialist Philosophy*, Benin City:
Skylight Prints, p. 4.
[24]. J.I. Omoregbe, (1991), *A Simplified History of Western Philosophy: Contemporary
Philosophy*, vol. 3, Lagos: Joja Educational Research and Publishers, p. 38.
[25]. B. Agidigbi, p. 4.
[26]. M. Heidegger, (1956), "The Way Back into the Ground of Metaphysics" in
W. Kaufmaun, (ed.), *Existentialism from Dostoevski to Sartre*, New York: Meridian
Books, p. 215.

Existentialism developed as a philosophical movement to assist man find solutions to the problems of his existence. To achieve this, it must and does involve many aspects of the existence of man. Therefore, William Barret defines it as "a philosophy that confronts human situation in its totality, to ask what the basic conditions of human existence are and how man can establish his own meaning out of these conditions."[27] This definition implies that existentialism helps man to deal with his personal experiences as it stresses individuality, authenticity, anxiety, and freedom.[28] Samuel Stumpf describes existentialism as "a mode of philosophy which focuses upon the existing individual person; instead of searching for truth in distant universal concepts, existentialism is concerned with the authentic concerns of concrete existing individuals as they face choices and decisions in daily life."[29]

From the definitions above, we can easily outline the following as the questions that interest the existentialist:

    i.   What is life?
    ii.   What is the world?
    iii. What is man?
    iv. Who am I?
    v.   What is being?

The definitions above also enable us to grasp the popular maxim and cardinal tenet of existentialism that 'existence precedes essence.' This has been interpreted to mean that subjectivity should be the actual starting point of philosophy and that the focus of philosophy should be the individual instead of engaging in endless debates and arguments on the nature of reality.

---

[27] . W. Barret, (1962), *Philosophy in the 20th Century*, vol.3, New York: Random House, p. 143.
[28] . D. Nyong, p. 42.
[29] . S.E. Stumpf, (1989), *Philosophy: History and Problems*, 4th Ed. New York: McGraw Hill Inc. p. 920.

A Brief Historical Account of Existentialism

Existentialism as we have it in contemporary Western philosophy emerged in Paris after the Second World War. It began like a philosophical fad with practitioners expressing their views and opinions in *cafes* and not within the four-walls of universities where you have professional philosophers. Rather than this fad to pass into oblivion as most fads do, it persisted and gained momentum, finding its way into virtually every form of human thought and expressions, including the novel, theatre, poetry, art and theology. It goes on to achieve far wider response than any other mode of philosophy without any sign that it will wane.[30]

Under the Weimar Republic in Germany, existentialism was one of the major currents of thought with Heidegger and Jaspers among its leaders. Back in the middle of the 19th Century, Kierkegaard had already worked out its main themes, with variations in the works of Schelling and Marx. So many writers with different philosophical orientations became identified with existentialism, which explains the many forms of existentialism we have. We probably have more differences than similarities among existentialists' philosophers. What, however, all existentialist philosophers have in common is their concern about human existence; the conditions and quality of the existing human individual.[31]

According to Stumpf, existentialism as a philosophical movement was bound to happen. This is because, over the centuries, the individual was pushed to the background by different systems of thought, historical events, and technological forces. Prior to existentialism, philosophy had hardly paid attention to the uniquely personal concerns of individuals. It had rather dwelt on the technical issues of metaphysics, ethics, and epistemology in general and objective manner, such that the intimate concerns of individuals about their personal identity were bypassed. The same story of disregard for the feelings and aspirations of individuals was observed in historical events, especially wars. Technology, which was initially supposed to aid man, gathered its own momentum and forced individuals to fit their lives into its own rhythm of machines rather

---

[30] . Ibid., p. 474.
[31] . Ibid., p. 475.

than the other way round. Therefore, the peculiarly human qualities of the individual were fading out. As Stumpf puts it, "they [individuals] were being converted from 'persons' into 'pronouns,' from 'subjects' into 'objects,' from an 'I' into an 'it'."[32]

Even religion that traditionally emphasizes the sense of worth and meaning of man and thus offers guidance began to suffer from the impact of rational and scientific thought. This increased the sense of worthlessness and meaninglessness in life. Against this growing sense of worthlessness and meaninglessness, some existentialist philosophers took an atheistic position, while some others turned still to religion to rediscover what they believed had been lost in the face of rational and scientific thinking. But be they atheistic or theistic, existentialist philosophers shared the same view that traditional Western philosophy was too academic and removed from life and therefore not giving any adequate meaning to man and his existence.

Against this current, existentialism favours a more subjective and individualistic approach to the concerns of human existence. It aims at improving the conditions of human existence, adding quality to human life. It is an effort to re-awaken self-realization and self-actualization of the individual; to help redeem him from the 'pronouns' and 'objects' he has been turned into by the overly rational and scientific thought systems of traditional Western philosophy. As it were, existentialism tries to make man live as persons by helping man to achieve an authentic personal existence. While denying objective universal values, it argues that man must create values for himself through his actions by living to its full each moment. If you like, you can call it a philosophy of 'the now.' To achieve this aim, existentialism uses what is referred to as the phenomenological method.

---

[32] . Ibid.

Chapter

2

Themes in Existentialism

Introduction

A perceptive study of the writings of existentialists shows that some
themes are easily identifiable in their works. These themes are
grounded on the human existential experience, informed by the
conditions within which human life and existence are situated. These
themes have to do with the factors that limit the individual. They are
the natural imperatives upon which human existence revolves. They
include the responsibilities upon the individual, which is a product of
the choices the human being has to make. These are the issues,
according to existentialists, that define human existence and place
upon the human being the responsibility of shaping the world even
within the difficulties that limit his possibilities. These difficulties,
real as they are, do not provide any excuse for human failure. Below
we shall examine the concepts with which existentialists articulate
their views about human existence.

Existence Precedes Essence

The thesis that 'existence precedes essence' is central to
existentialism. It means that the most important consideration for the
individual is the fact that he or she is an individual.[33] This proposition
reverses "the traditional philosophical view that the essence or the

---

[33] . "Existentialism" in www.en.wikipedia.org/wiki/Existentialism#Existence
_ precedes_essence (Retrieved on 19/3/13).

nature of a thing is more fundamental and immutable than its existence." [34] By existence here we mean an agent that acts independently and is responsibly conscious of his or her being, and essence refers to roles, labels, stereotypes, definitions, or other preconceived categories that the individual fits into. Without the actual life of the individual, we cannot talk about his true essence, meaning that the actual life of the individual constitutes what we call his true essence.

Human beings, through their own consciousness, create their own values and determine a meaning to their life. Thus, the individual person defines himself or herself. The individual wishes to be something, this something can be anything, and then be the thing. The phrase, 'existence precedes essence' means that a person decides by his own actions, for which he is responsible, what he wants to be. For instance, when someone acts cruelly towards another, by virtue of the cruel act he or she is defined as a cruel person. By this very action of cruelty the person is responsible for his or her identity as a cruel person. The argument implies that, it is not gene or human nature that bestows on the individual his or her identity. The human person is neither cruel nor good, for instance, essentially, he or she makes a choice to act in a way that defines him or her as cruel or good. As Sartre puts it, "man first of all exists, encounters himself, surges up in the world – and defines himself afterwards."[35]

According to Sartre, we do not and cannot explain human nature as we would describe any other manufactured article. With regard to a manufactured article, we know someone manufactured it, how it was manufactured, what it was made from, the purpose for which it was manufactured and the eventual use of the article. It means that even before the article is manufactured, its purpose was defined and its process of manufacturing definitive. If essence refers to the purpose and procedure of manufacture, it means the article of manufacture has an essence that precedes its existence. The theist may conceive the human nature from this perspective in relation to God, but as for Sartre, if there is no God, there would not be a talk of a given human nature because there is no God to conceive it prior

---

[34] . Ibid (Retrieved 6/12/13).
[35] . Ibid.

to its existence. Indeed, Sartre insists that human nature cannot be defined in advance because it cannot be completely thought out in advance. He contends that the human being merely exists and later becomes his or her essential self. This implies that the human being is, first and foremost, and in the process of being, confronts him or herself and thereby defines him or herself. In summary, the human being is what he or she makes of him or herself.

Our first reaction to Sartre's formulation of this first principle of existentialism is to conceive it as very subjective. This is in the sense that the human being is seen as making him or herself anything he or she wishes. We should however, note that the primary aim of Sartre here is to emphasize that the dignity of the human being is greater than that of a mere stone or table and this dignity is bestowed on the human being by virtue of his or her subjective life. It implies that the human being consciously moves himself or herself towards the future. Inherent in Sartre's notion is the distinction between two modes of being, which he calls, *being-in-itself* (*l' en-soi*) and *being-for-itself* (*le poursoi*). In Sartre's view, the human being shares in these two different modes of being. The *being-in-itself* refers to the fact that the human being *is*, just like the stone or table, while the *being-for-itself* refers to the fact that the human being is a *conscious subject*, which differentiates him or her from a stone. A conscious subject is one who constantly stands before a future.

The implication of placing existence before essence by the existentialist is to emphasize the fact that the human being creates himself or herself, and more importantly, that he or she is solely responsible for his or her existence. This would be impossible if the human being's essential nature were fixed and given. The latter would make the human being just like the stone, which cannot be responsible for itself.

Man

Man, in the context of our discussion, refers to the human being as an individual. Man is a self-transcending being according to existentialism. He is a conscious being who always projects into the future; he goes beyond his present, looking into and projecting into the future. Existentialism contends that man should be the central focus of philosophy; he is not to be thought of in terms of his essence or as a form as Plato's philosophy argued. Man is what he is according to how he makes himself. Against Plato's idea that a man is a man by virtue of his participation in *manness* as in the world of forms, existentialism argues that man is a self-creating being. He first exists, and then makes himself what he is because existence precedes essence.

Existentialism places possibilities over necessities. It sees man's existence as a possibility and in this possibility lies reality, that is, the reality of man. Sartre argues that things, events, persons and their relations present themselves as possibilities and not as necessities.[36]

Man is a unique individual who is a self-conscious being. He has his own irreversible history and he is not replaceable in the society. He also has an interiority that is impenetrable but can only be accessed by him. His self-consciousness and impenetrable interiority constitute his subjectivity. This view is against man's conception of himself as strictly a member of the society who believes society makes him what he is. To think that society makes you what you are is to fail to see yourself as an individual who must determine your own destiny; as in what you want to be. Thinking of oneself as just a member of society allows oneself to drift with and be drifted by the majority; this makes one anonymous and lost in the crowd and at loss with the crowd. Issues are decided on the basis of majority opinion, which makes man unable to stand out in any unusual way. To allow the above is to make man a machine in the hands of society.

As a result of the above, existentialists demonstrate an antipathy towards the anonymous featureless standards which prevail in society. Hence, they feel the need for a philosophy that is directed towards the internal edification of the individual self. This is a kind of personalist philosophy.

Such a personalist philosophy will conceive man as a self-transcending being who goes beyond what he is at the moment and looks towards the future; this makes him different from other beings. He is self-conscious, lives a unique life, irreplaceable; lives his life and dies his death. Man is not an objectifiable subject or fixed entity, he is an individual who is responsible for his decisions and actions.

---

[36] . D. Nyong, p. 43.

Man and the World

Here existentialism is concerned with the relationship between man
and the world. Existentialists evaluate the world in the light of an
examination of the relationship of the being in the world and not in
the light of knowledge or perception. For the existentialists, the
existence of the world is a matter of course and man and the world
are inseparable. This is because, as a conscious and existent being,
man does not exist in a vacuum; man is a part of the world and
cannot exist without the world. The reality of the world is attached
to the existence of man. Man's existence is, therefore, attached to the
world in which he lives. Man is not just a thing in the world; he is an
inseparable part of the world. Within this context, the existentialists
see the attempt to prove the existence of the world as a scandal, since
a failure to will be a contradiction while to succeed will be
tautologous. Even to use the phrase, 'external world' is unacceptable
to existentialists since such a phrase makes the world autonomous
and therefore, an objective reality apart from man. Man, the thinker,
is, and should be made part of the object of thought. While science
sees man as a disinterested observer and objective spectator,
philosophy should adopt the sharply different methodology of
making man a part and parcel of the world that he observes and
perceives.

The question of proving the existence of the world should not be
raised at all as it is a given, for man who raises the question is part
and parcel of the world, he does not exist except within the universe.
Therefore, the very fact of man's existence already presupposes the
existence of the world. Existence, for existentialists, is having one's
being as a human individual in the world.[37] Though the individual is
self-conscious, his consciousness is a consciousness of something and
it, *ipso facto*, implies a world in general. The human mode of being
necessarily implies a world.

According to Heidegger, man is a being-in-the-world. He does not
become aware of himself alone, but becomes aware of himself in the
world and controlled by the world. The world is not independent of
those who talk about it; it includes the point of view of the person

---

[37] . Ibid., p. 45.

who is talking about it and the totality of his environment as he is aware of it.[38] The world is a necessary constituent of existence; no world, no existence. Without the world there is no self and to exist is to be in a world and stand out from the world. As Sartre puts it, there is no world without selfhood and without the world there is no selfhood.[39]

The body is the link between man and the world since it is through the body that man comes in contact with the world as well as interacts with the world. Though it is true that humans exist in the world, they however transcend the world. There is the tendency for man to be completely absorbed in the world. Man should resist this tendency. If he does not, he ceases to exist as man and becomes just a thing, an article or object among other objects surrounding him in the world. Man gives the world its value and meaning, as the world exists for man and man uses it as a means for self-fulfilment. Man lives in the world; he finds a home in the world and cares for the world. The being of man is fundamentally constituted in the world to which he, as man, is inextricably and unavoidably bound.

The world is always a world of man since it receives its meaning and interpretative reality from man; to talk about the world is to talk about man at the same time. The expression 'world' implies the human stand-point from which everything is seen. Man, therefore, cannot be considered in isolation from the world or *vice versa*. Man realizes his being as 'being-in-the-world,' and therefore, we can say that man and the world are in a mutualistic symbiosis.[40] Man and the world form a totality in which they are related to each other by a series of 'in-orderto.'

Man and the Others

Existentialism maintains that the existence of the individual necessarily implies the existence of others, for the individual cannot exist without the others. This means that man is not only a being-in-the-world but also a being-with-others.

---

[38] . J. Macquarrie, p. 79.
[39] . J. P. Sartre, (1956), *Being and Nothingness*, New York: Methuen and Company Ltd., p. 104.
[40] . D. Nyong, p. 47.

Although existentialism, like Cartesianism, emphasizes individual subjectivity, it, however, unlike Cartesianism, insists that awareness of self is not in isolation; for when a man discovers himself, he also discovers the world and the others. According to Sartre, "in the *cogito* one does not discover only oneself but others as well ... thus, the man who attains himself directly through the *cogito*, discovers all others also."[41]

Existentialists stress the social nature of man as a being-with-others, while maintaining man's individuality, singularity, and uniqueness. This implies that the individual should not allow himself to be lost in the crowd of the 'they.' In the light of this, existentialists make a distinction between authentic and inauthentic existence.

The authentic life or existence is the life lived by the free choice of the individual. Herein the individual is fully aware of his own freedom, which enables him to make choices and assume full responsibility for his choices. It implies that the individual should not simply drift along with the crowd; a situation where he does things because others are doing them or just because it is the custom of the place. Authenticity, therefore, preserves the individual identity from the erosion of societal influences and demands. On the contrary, the inauthentic life or existence is the life lived according to the dictates of another man. In this case, the individual is not living his life but the life dictated to him by the other person. Inauthenticity denies the individual's liberty as he dances to the tune of society without questioning its validity.

According to Martin Buber, the very fact of the individual's coming into the world is tantamount to coming into being-with-others. Therefore, as he realizes himself as an individual, he equally realizes the others. This expresses the social nature of man with other beings. Life is meaningful in relation to the others as our actions only make meaning as they relate and affect other people.[42]

---

[41] . J. I. Omoregbe, p. 44.
[42] . D. Nyong, p. 50.

Freedom, Choice and Responsibility

Freedom is one of the cardinal issues for the existentialist philosophers. As MacIntyre puts it, "if any single thesis could be said to constitute the doctrine of existentialism, it would be that the possibility of choice is the central fact of human nature."[43] Freedom, for the existentialist, is part of the structure of the being of man and therefore a basic condition of his existence. It is not a property but part of the very structure of man. Man, by virtue of his existence, is condemned to be free; freedom is identical with his existence and as such it is not something he acquires. An attempt to prove that man is free is an attempt to prove that man exist, the latter is obviously absurd.

Freedom for man is tied to choice. Freedom is freedom to choose, meaning that freedom and choice are inseparably bound. Choice is the concrete actualization of freedom. Freedom compels man to assume responsibility for his life; that is, to take his destiny in his hands. Human freedom is freedom to choose and not freedom not to choose. As a matter of fact, not to choose is actually to choose not to choose, which is equivalent to making a choice in itself.

Man's future is not marked out *a priori*, he has a virgin future which he is free to live out as he wants. It is like a blank canvass before the artist who is free to paint whatever he wants on it. No indications to direct man's movement into his future, he is free to follow any direction of his choice and therefore, shape for himself his life as he wants. He however, takes responsibility for whatever choices he makes and whatever directions he decides to take. Thus, he is responsible for whatever he becomes in life.[44] According to Sartre, "... the first step of existentialism is to put the whole man in possession of what he is and to make the total responsibility of his existence to rest on him."[45]

Existentialists ascribe a radical freedom to man, but this radical freedom carries with it a total responsibility without the possibility of an excuse. There are, however, limitations to human freedom and

[43] . A. A. MacIntyre, (1967), "Existence and Essence" in *The Encyclopedia of Philosophy*, vol. 3 and 4, London: Macmillan and Free Press, p. 149.
[44] . B. Agidigbi, p. 24.
[45] . J. P. Sartre, (1970), *L'Existentialismest un Humanisnism*, Paris: Nagel, p. 24.

activities laid on it by history and society.[46] This means there are obstacles to human freedom everywhere. It is notable to immediately add that these obstacles are equally the products of freedom itself. This implies that freedom suffers from its own self-imposed restrictions. These restrictions notwithstanding, man is still free, for freedom is identical with his being and existence.

Freedom should be distinguished from accomplishment; that man is free does not mean he always accomplishes whatever he wants to do. Freedom is not 'will to power.' While freedom is the permanent ability to choose, as in, decide for oneself what to do, accomplishment is the realization of what one chooses to do. That one is able to make a choice to be something other than another thing, does not necessarily translate to the fact that one becomes the thing he chooses to be and not the other. This, however, does not remove the exercise of one's freedom. Therefore, if one is not able to accomplish what he has chosen to do, he would still have exercised his freedom to choose as he makes the choice of what to do.

According to Nyong,

> Man's possession of freedom makes him unpredictable, since he can never be identified with anything in particular nor identified with any particular way of life. The existentialist philosophers maintain that man is not and cannot be anything in a fixed, permanent way, since he can always change. Man's freedom puts him above the past, the environment, the rules of language and the dialectics of history. Man by his freedom confers meaning to the world and life itself. Man uses his freedom to designate meaning to things in the world.[47]

This accounts for man's dynamic nature, for he can always be this today and something other than this tomorrow. For instance, a man can choose to be humane and kind-hearted today to X and tomorrow chooses to be cruel and unyielding to X. His freedom to choose makes him unpredictable for until he does what he chooses to do, we

---

[46] . J. I. Omoregbe, p. 48.
[47] . D. Nyong, p. 53.

can only at best presume, based on informed or educated guess that he will act in a particular way or otherwise.

Facticity

Facticity refers to the limiting factors of human existence. Many writers criticize the existentialists for ascribing absolute freedom to man, while we are very much aware of physiological and psychological factors, environmental constitutions, and conditions of human birth, to mention a few, that determine the situations in man's life for which he cannot take responsibility. These factors militate against human freedom and man cannot, therefore, be held wholly responsible for all he does.

The above criticism forces Sartre and other existentialists to concede to each man his facticity. Facticity has to do with the awareness of man's finitude; his inability to know beyond what he can know. It deals with the limiting factors of human existence. Man is not the author of his life but he is forced to take responsibility for his mode of being. He is thrown into the world and he has to contend with death, decay, sickness, disappointments, sorrow, and incapacitations. These constitute limitations to man's freedom; they constitute the facticity of human existence. According to Sartre, facticity has to do with psychological limitations that we impose upon ourselves. When we surmount these psychological limitations that constitute facticity, we affirm our authentic existence.

In Sartre's opinion, man is thrown into the world without consultation; he is just a person and no other, he is of a particular sex and not the other, race, colour, heredity, intelligence quotient, temperament, of a particular historical situation, etc. This makes man limited and empty. He carries the emptiness within himself and tries, often in vain, all through his life, to fill this emptiness. Facticity, therefore, leaves man a victim who exists without knowing where he comes from and where he is going to.

That man does not know where he is coming from and where he is going to is highly contestable in the face of religious faiths, mythologies and beliefs in creation that try to establish the origin of man as an article of faith. No matter what the disputes may be on this issue, the fact remains according to Desan, "that we are thrown into the world without explanation or justification that we are in a way abandoned."[48]

Facticity explains the limits and boundaries that we cannot go beyond or transcend; it does not however stop us from making efforts or overcoming our shortcomings, so as to take control and charge over them. This will in turn enable us reach the full realization of our essence and being. Therefore, Donceel writes:

> But this [facticity] does not rob me of initiative or freedom. But it sets down a framework within which my liberty will have to be exercised.[49]

This expresses the fact that man has no unlimited possibility; instead, his possibility is limited by the situation of his facticity.

Anguish [*Angst*]

Anguish, or its German equivalent *Angst*, is very pivotal to existentialism. According to Heidegger, it "provides the phenomenal basis for explicitly grasping *Dasein*'s primodial totality of being."[50] As a theme, anguish is common to all existentialists and it comes across as one of the characteristic features of human existence. It is, at times expressed as 'anxiety' or 'dread.' It refers to the uneasiness that man faces whenever he has to make a decision. It comes with reflection on the absurdities, nothingness and finality of human existence. It is something that is borne out of the fact of choice. Man's awareness and realization of his freedom to choose between alternatives makes him apprehensive of the responsibilities that go with his freedom of choice.

Sartre describes anguish as a sense of "complete and profound responsibility [which a person feels, when] fully realizing that he is not only choosing what he will be, but ... deciding for the whole of mankind."[51] This is not to be confused with fear. In fact, anguish and

---

[48] . W. Desan, (1954), *The Tragic Final*, Cambridge: University Press, p. 108.
[49] . J. F. Donceel, (1967), *Philosophical Anthropology*, New York: Kansas, p. 458.
[50] . M. Heidegger, (1962), *Being and Time*, Oxford: Blackwell Publishers, p. 182H.
[51] . J. P. Sartre, *Existentialism and Humanism*, p. 30.

fear are not the same thing. While the object of anguish lies within; it is in the nature of man, the object of fear is outside of man; fear is caused by an external thing. For instance, when we are afraid, it is always of something outside of us that we are afraid of. Anguish is the recognition of a possibility as our possibility. It is not avoidable and cannot be hidden. The anguish of man in his decision-making process is not because he is free to choose but because he is responsible for his choice.

Death

Existentialists pay attention to death because they are convinced that death reveals the authentic possibilities of human existence. Their discourse on death is more like a continuation of that of anguish. For them, anguish arises in relation to one's death. According to Heidegger, "Being-towards-death is essentially anguish." [52] This implies that, although death is not the object of anguish, the prospect of death, however, gives rise to anguish towards its object, namely, 'being-in-the-world.' So, we should not understand anguish as the fear of death.

The concern of existentialist about death is not about the way it comes, but about the finitude of existence. That is, the very fact that existence ends. The existentialist is also not particularly concerned with the event of death itself, he is, rather, concerned with human life in relation to the prospect of the event of death. Thus, Heidegger refers to death as an 'existential phenomenon.' According to him, "when we speak of death, it does not signify *Dasein's* Being-at-an-end ... but a *Being-towards-the-end* ... death is a way to be."[53]

The existentialist gives the impression that death gives meaning to life. Montaigne had the popular dictum, which De Beauvoir notes with approval, that, "the continuous work of life is to build death."[54]In his own words, Jaspers refers to death as "throwing us back upon the fulfillment of *Existenz*."[55] Thus, the existentialist opines

---

[52] . M. Heidegger, *Being and Time*, p. 266H.
[53] . Ibid., p. 245H.
[54] . S. D. Beauvoir, (1948), *The Ethics of Ambiguity*, Citadel, p. 7.
[55] . K. Jaspers, (1969-71), *Philosophy*, vol. 2, Chicago: University of Chicago Press, p. 200.

that death is responsible for giving meaning to existence. This should not be understood in the Christian sense of death being a gateway to a better life in the presence of God. Death or finitude for the existentialist is the final end of life. For the existentialist, if death has meaning, it is precisely as the end, the final end, of life.

There are three reasons why the existentialist thinks that the phenomenon of death gives rise to anguish:

i.   A person's finitude is at least a necessary condition of his freedom and individuality

ii. Attention to a particular aspect of a person's fate after death throws into sharper relief how things stand with him when alive.

iii. The anticipation of death utterly individualizes *Dasein*.[56]

The third reason (iii) above is most important to the existentialist. A person is individualized when he withdraws from getting immersed in the crowd or the world of the others and lending a wholeness and integrity to his life. In the opinion of Heidegger, when one anticipates death, he is "wrenched away from the 'they'" and therefore, liberates himself from the lostness to the crowd. Getting lost to the crowd thrust accidental possibilities upon the individual, from which getting freed from the crowd, in anticipation of death relieves one.

---

[56] . D. E. Cooper, pp. 134-136.

Chapter

3

Key Existentialist Thinkers

Soren Kierkegaard (1813-1855)

Kierkegaard is considered as the father of modern existentialism because he was the first to express many of the themes of contemporary existentialism. He was not just a philosopher; he was also a religious writer, psychologist, journalist, and literary critic. Amongst his works are: *Fear and Trembling, Either/Or, Philosophical Fragments, Stages on Life's Way,* and *Concluding Unscientific Postscript.*

Kierkegaard opines that the history of thought is preoccupied by wrong concerns. According to him, from the earliest times of philosophy, philosophy has paid too much attention on architectonic metaphysical schemes, over esteeming either reason or experience to provide us knowledge of the world. Unfortunately, neither rationalism nor empiricism, as systems of inquiry, takes into account the fundamental human condition. We are always faced with the need to make decisions; therefore, choice is always our point of departure, our constant companion, and the heaviest burden we bear.

Kierkegaard's philosophy is considered a reaction to Hegel's attempt to bring the whole of reality, human beings inclusive, within his conceptual system. This fact is obvious in his work, *Either/Or,* which is primarily a treatise against Hegelianism. As far as Hegel was concerned, a thing is only meaningful if it is a part of a whole, nothing viewed in isolation of the whole is real but an illusion. Kierkegaard found Hegel's philosophy comical because in his great efforts to capture all of reality in his system of thought, he left out the most important element of existence. According to Stumpf, "what made Hegel comic for Kierkegaard was that this great philosopher had tried to capture all of reality in his system of thought, yet in the process lost the most important element, namely, *existence*."[57]

Kierkegaard treated the term "existence" as a word reserved for individual human being. To exist is to be a certain kind of individual who strives and considers alternatives; he chooses, decides, and commits himself to his choices and decisions. Neither choice, nor decisions, nor commitments were implied in the works of Hegel. This omission of Hegel led Kierkegaard to reject systematization and objectivity in favor of subjectivity. He considered objectivity as impersonal and subjectivity as personal. Subjectivity, being personal, entails self-commitment. According to Stumpf, "Kierkegaard's whole career might well be considered as a self-conscious revolt against abstract thought and an attempt on his part to live up to Feuerbach's admonition: "Do not wish to be a philosopher in contrast to being a man ... do not think as a thinker ... think as a living, real being ... think in Existence."[58]

Kierkegaard considers truth as subjectivity, since truth is bound to existential appropriation. According to him, "for existing, striving, deciding persons there is not available 'out there' a pre-fabricated truth." [59] In his opinion, what is out there is "an objective uncertainty." This seems more like an anticipation of William James' view of "truth is made." For him, the important question about truth is whether it is true for me and am I prepared to live by it and commit myself to it rather than whether it is objective or not. He considers 'personal choice', 'freedom', 'commitment', 'personal responsibility', etc. as key terms. The point Kierkegaard is making here is that people should realize what it means to exist and be a Christian.

For Kierkegaard, religious belief is the answer to the problem of choice when we are faced with making decisions. Religious belief is not a matter of reason but one of passion. Reason undermines faith and can never justify it. Getting involved in rationalistic proofs of God's existence, for instance, does not necessarily bring about belief

---

[57] . S. E. Stumpf, p. 476.
[58] . Ibid., pp. 476-477.
[59] . Ibid., p. 479.

in God. To believe in God is a matter of choice and not an intellectual exercise. As Philip Stokes puts it, for Kierkegaard,

> An authentic belief acquires its force from within, as a 'leap of faith' without the guidance of reason to reassure us that what we are doing is 'right' or 'true.' Such reassurances, would, after all, maintains Kierkegaard, remove the need for faith if God's existence were simply a matter of commonsense or rational reflection.[60]

In his description of the existential situation of man, Kierkegaard distinguishes between man's present state, which is what he is now, and what he ought to be, or what he is essentially. He, therefore, argues for a movement in the life of man from the essential to the existential; that is, from what he ought to be to what he is now. The essential nature of man involves his relation to the infinite, which is God, while the existential nature of man is a consequence of his alienation from the infinite. Alienation from the infinite, which is God, arises from the individual losing himself in the crowd. The crowd, for Kierkegaard, is 'untruth' and it makes the individual impenitent and irresponsible. This is irrespective of the kind of crowd; be it a rich or poor crowd, a political crowd or even a church congregation.

In his Christian faith, Kierkegaard sees the individual immersed in the crowd as an attempt by the individual to derive meaning for his existence. This is, however, a wrong attempt; the right attempt is to relate oneself with God instead of any other thing. In the eyes of God, humankind do not constitute a crowd, for God sees each individual as an individual within the society. Therefore, man continues to live a life full of anxiety until he actualizes his essential self in God. His anxiety is a result of the fact that while he lives existentially, he is alienated from his essential self. This alienation in turn creates a dynamic drive in man to discover his essential self.

To explain this dynamic drive or movement in the life of a person, Kierkegaard outlines three levels or stages of existence; namely,

---

[60] . P. Stokes (2012). *Philosophy: 100 Essential Thinkers,* London: Arcturus Publishing Ltd., p. 264.

   i.   Aesthetic stage
   ii. Ethical stage
   iii. Religious stage

At the aesthetic stage man drifts from pleasure to pleasure. He, however, soon discovers that life at this level does not produce the authentic self, and therefore, would not result in true existence. He is now faced with the 'either – or.' That is, either he remains on the level of aesthetic with its fatal attractions or he moves to the next stage.

At the ethical level, man recognizes and accepts rules of conduct formulated from reason. He however comes to realize later that he is not capable of fulfilling the moral law, which he finds himself violating deliberately. Conscious of the fact that he deliberately violates the rules of conduct, he develops a sense of guilt, which in turn becomes an antithesis that brings him face to face with the 'either – or' question again. Either he remains with his sense of guilt at the ethical level, or he confronts the new reality; his awareness of the guilt.

The third stage; the religious level, comes to be as the individual tries to confront his awareness of his guilt. At this point, he is faced with the reality of the existence of God and the awareness of his self-alienation. Thus, he realizes more clearly the need to find self-fulfillment in God. At the religious stage, the individual becomes aware that to become his authentic self he must commit himself to God. The point of Kierkegaard's argument is that authentic existence is not a result of the intellect but rather a matter of faith and commitment. Commitment involves a continuous process of choice making in the face of the varieties of 'either – or.'

This brief exposé of Kierkegaard's existential thought implies that the individual's freedom is based on his ability to think for himself without necessarily falling back on conventions or institutionalized moral codes of conduct. The individual's freedom is tantamount to isolation, because he is solely responsible for his decision on how he wants to live. To be free means to be a man of his own, his own master. As his own master, he decides within his own creativity what is valuable and what is not valuable. The authentic man for Kierkegaard is the man who has nothing to do with universal or societal moral codes. His morality is to the extent that he personally discovers the truth.[61]

Friedrich Nietzsche (1844-1900)

Nietzsche, who had prophetically predicted that his name will be associated with something monstrous, is the son of a Lutheran pastor. He announced the death of God. He was a very profound and enigmatic philosopher, who also turned out to be very controversial. As a philosopher, he was variously appropriated; vilified, venerated or simply misunderstood. [62] He was a thorough-going atheistic existentialist. He understood philosophy and addressed philosophical issues from the point of view of the conflict of the age rather than the disputes between the various thought systems in the universities. His works are varied and treats various topics, ranging from ethics and religion to metaphysics and epistemology. He is, however, mostly renowned for his concept of "the will to power".

According to him, the individual's fundamental driving force is expressed in his need to dominate and control the external forces prevailing upon him. Therefore, the individual requires the power to be the master of his own destiny. Failure or frustration to realize this urge is the reason for the existence of the various moral systems and religious institutions we have. These moral systems and religious institutions attempt to subdue and bind our will. For Nietzsche, the will to power is to be pursued and affirmed rather than something to be resisted. The will to power is the affirmation of life.

He launched a vehement attack against Christianity because he saw it as a religious institution that tries to subdue and bind the power to will. According to him, Christianity as a system does many deplorable things in the name of God, claiming to hand down the commands and prohibitions of God to man. He argued against absolute objectivity of morality and proposed that there are two kinds of morality:

i.   The slave morality
ii.   The master morality.

---

[61] . B. Agidigbi, pp. 29-34.
[62] . P. Stokes, p. 266.

The slave morality stems from Christianity. This is the kind of morality that teaches love, meekness, self-denial, etc. It glorifies weakness as a virtue and deplores strength of character as a vice. The aim of slave morality is basically to bring men to the same level by subjecting them to absolute and universal laws. This is an obstacle to the development of man.

Against slave morality, Nietzsche pronounced God dead and argued that the death of God is the freedom of man. For him, the death of God sets humanity free from the enslaving and oppressive, absolute and universal commandments and prohibitions, which inhibit human growth and development. With the death of God, the slave morality gives way to the master morality.

The master morality is that of the man who takes over the place of God. He becomes the legislator of moral laws. The man who takes over is the man who has rejected the values of the slave morality and has reversed the values. This is what Nietzsche called the '*transvaluation*' of values. In the *transvaluation* of values, master morality becomes a morality of power, ruthlessness, struggle, and ambition.

The 'superman' is the ideal man who embodies the master morality. The superman is above and beyond good and evil as he creates his own values. Having liberated himself from the enslaving morality of the reign of God, which is tied to the belief in God, he evolves his own values and morality. Dostoyevsky had argued that if God is dead, it would mean that all things are now permitted. Nietzsche picked up this implication and developed it thus; no absolute values, therefore, each individual must create and develop his own values. He does this in relation to the tasks he sets for himself. To pronounce God dead is to reject God as the basis of our values, therefore, man has to source a new basis for his values and he must make himself that new basis of his own values. This implies that man decides for himself what is valuable, what is meaningful, and what is true.

The consequence of the death of God is that the old morality disappears and everything is now permissible. This further reveals nihilism, emptiness, nothingness, and meaninglessness in human existence. This gains support in Nietzsche's doctrine of the eternal recurrence of all things. This doctrine holds that there is a continuous process of endless repetition of things. Implied in this doctrine is the fact that anything happening now had happened in the past and will happen again in the future. Human existence, for Nietzsche is part and parcel of this eternal recurrence. According to him, it is an "eternal process of endless, purposeless, and meaningless repetition".[63] This means human life or existence has no meaning, no purpose, no aim, and no goal.

Nietzsche's existentialist philosophy can be interpreted in various ways and forms. Some of such possible interpretations are:

i.   It is a philosophy that encourages or teaches violence, brutality, selfishness, immorality, and other vices.

ii.   It is a philosophy that encourages a remarkable drive for man to free himself from any form of bondage.

iii.   It is a philosophy that attempts to breed the real and authentic man. Authenticity here is used in the sense of not allowing oneself to get drowned in the beliefs of the 'foolish' majority.

The third interpretation (iii) above is understood as an "emotional crusade", which is needed to launch man into the stage of enlightenment and fast-track him into new possibilities. Man must, however, take responsibility for his actions.

In comparism to Kierkegaard, whose efforts were to turn man back to God as an authentic Christian in order to discover and live his existential and essential life to the full, Nietzsche frantically wants man to reject God and chat his own path in order to discover and live his authentic life.

Martin Heidegger (1889-1976)

Heidegger was a central figure in the formulation and propagation of existentialism. He did not develop a set of ideas or a system of philosophy, neither can it be said that he produced anything in the way of a neat structure of academic ideas, he was not so much interested in objects of scholarship. However, "with one bold stroke",

---

[63] . Ibid., p. 37.

according to Stumpf, "he shifted the attention of twentieth-century Continental philosophy away from traditional concerns about theories and books and focused instead upon the concerns of thinking individual."[64]

An individual is born in the world and responds to all his experiences by thinking. What Heidegger set out to explore was the deepest nature of an individual's thinking when he is thinking as an existing human being.[65]

Having been introduced to philosophy at the young age of seventeen through the reading of Franz Brentano's *On the Manifold Meaning of Being according to Aristotle*, he took on the lifelong endeavour to search for the meaning of being, which for him, is the meaning that reigns in everything that is. He was also influenced by Kierkegaard, Dostoyevsky, and Nietzsche. His book, *Being and Time*, published in 1927, was regarded as the fundamental source of modern existentialism. It was a very influential book.

Heidegger's contribution to philosophy has been very influential. In his opinion, the history of philosophy was concerned with the wrong questions. From the time of Plato, philosophers have been asking questions about what there is and what can be known about that which is. These questions presuppose too much; they presuppose too much of dualism. By dualism, we mean a state or system of two essential parts. Within the context of our immediate discussion, we have, for instance, the Cartesian dualism of the subject and the object (external world). Heidegger rejects this division and indeed, the notion that there is a world external to some conscious spectator. He rather thinks that philosophy should focus on "What is Being?" rather than the various dualisms that characterize the history of philosophy. For him, the question "what is being?" is a suggestion that we examine, first and foremost, what it means for a thing to 'be' before we begin to examine the properties that objects are made of. The question, "what is being?" arises from the most basic philosophical puzzle, namely, why is there something, instead of nothing? The question, "what is being?" generally narrows down to what type of

---

[64] . S. E. Stumpf, p. 496.
[65] . Ibid.

being one is. Therefore, he centers his inquiry on being, which he refers to as *Dasein*.

Heidegger was primarily concerned with clarifying our understanding of our own being. He tried to explain the meaning of being itself. He "transformed the concept of being from a highly abstract and remote concept into a subject of intense concern to every human being".[66] In doing this, he evolved a new vocabulary and gave new meanings to old words in order to pass across his philosophical thought. He had a fresh interpretation of the concept of being and evolved a new conception and understanding of man.

Heidegger sought to correct the error of thinking about man in the same way we think about things. He argued that there is a fundamental difference between man and things. Only man, for him, can raise the question about his being or about being itself. Things cannot do that. Generally, we think about things by defining them. Defining them consists in listing their attributes and characteristics. The essence of man cannot, however, be accounted for in this way. This is because the being of man includes his awareness of his being, which is not the same with the being of things.

According to Heidegger, the word 'man' can be deceptive because the history of philosophy defined man the way things are defined. For instance, Descartes thinks of man as mind and body, placing emphasis on man as a combination of two substances – mind and body. This understanding of man sets him off as a knowing subject that faces a world as a known or knowable object.[67] Heidegger opines that this is a distortion of the view of man and the world. Against this view, he seeks to avoid a definition of man in terms of properties or attributes that will divide man from the world. To achieve his aim, he coined a new word that he argues more accurately describes the experience of human existence. The word is *Dasein*.

Dasein is a German word which literally means 'being there', and as used technically by Heidegger, it means 'human existence.' Man as *Dasein* is a continuous being, who thinks about the meaning of everything that is. He is not seeking any particular result in his thought, he just thinks because he is a thinking or musing being. As

---

[66]. Ibid. p. 497.
[67]. B. Agidigbi, pp. 38-39.

Agidigbi puts it, *Dasein* "connotes that man is a being who is present to the world but whose presence is not just like that of a spatial object like the stone or hammer with a fixed nature but in the sense of a meaning-making-being-in-the-world".[68] Therefore, for Heidegger, the essence of man is not in attributes or properties but in how he exists. *Dasein* expresses a mode of understanding; it is like saying 'she is *in* love', which does not refer to the location of the 'she' but her mode of being, in the same way, man as '*Dasein*', that is, 'man as being-in-theworld,' is a description of the structure of his existence. This structure of his existence makes it possible for him to think meaningfully about the world.[69]

The term *Dasein* conveys a dynamic view of personality against the fixed nature or essence that the traditional conception of man has ascribed to him. Man as being is a possibility to become what he is not yet. So, man can be described as a being that is not yet what he is and a being that is more than he actually is at any given moment. This implies that man is not a finished product but a product in the process of becoming. Man is, therefore, essentially a free being who decides for himself his mode of being.

Man is being-in-the-world; therefore he is inseparable with the world of things and people. He is, however, essentially different from the things around him in the world. He knows the things around him in terms of their utility to him in his pursuit of his concerns. The world is therefore, an instrumental world for man and not an extension, as Descartes conceives it. Since by nature man is a social being, he is a being-with-others. He cannot live or be conceived in isolation.

Heidegger, in the first part of his very influential work, *Being and Time*, made an analysis of human existential traits. Here he discussed the existence of *Dasein* in three fundamental parts. According to him, man is characterized by three basic features. They are:

i.   Facticity
ii.   Existentiality
iii. Fallenness

---

[68] . Ibid., p. 39.
[69] . S. E. Stumpf, p. 498.

Facticity reveals the limitations of man. These limitations consist in the fact that man is thrown into a world without his consent. This implies that man is not responsible for his being-in-the-world. He just finds himself in existence and in circumstances that are not his own making. However, even though he is not responsible for his being-in-the-world and the circumstances surrounding his existence, he must freely put or install order in the world.

Existentiality describes man's possibility. This is the possibility of making himself what he wants to be. It includes also the possibility of changing the world by projecting himself into the future and committing himself to live in view of his self-project.

Fallenness describes man's tendency to alienate himself from his true or authentic self and makes him live an inauthentic life. As the world is the instrument for the formation of man, it is also the instrument for his alienation or fallenness; it can be responsible for his despair and sense of loss. This happens when man forgets his being and replaces it with other beings, that is, the crowd; he becomes lost to the world.

These three ontological features of man represent his present, past and future. Facticity refers to his past, fallenness refers to his present, and existentiality refers to his future. These are the three basic dimensions of time. This immediately brings out the fact that for Heidegger, to be authentic or live the authentic life, man must be conscious of the temporal nature of his existence. He must be aware and conscious of his possibilities in the past which is repeatable, his possibilities in the future which he anticipates and shapes by his free choices and decisions in the present. The present is therefore his moment of decision and vision. When man sees and appreciates himself in these three-tier temporal dimensions, he attains integrity and authenticity.

Jean-Paul Sartre (1905-1980)

Sartre made existentialism popular to the extent that existentialism became almost synonymous with his philosophy. His version of existentialism is a mix of three modes of thought that are associated with Marx, Husserl, and Heidegger. Common to these three modes of thought is the concern about man's active role in molding his own destiny. Marx had argued that philosophers have understood the world but the important point is to change it, while Husserl had argued that philosophy should seek its foundation in man; in the essence of man's concrete existence, and Heidegger had argued that our basic understanding of being is best achieved through the existential analysis of man. According to Stokes, "Sartre's philosophy possesses a clarity and force that captured the spirit of his time in a far more powerful way than that of either his predecessors or his existentialist contemporaries." [70] Sartre formulated his existential thought in his *Being and Nothingness* (1956). Prominent among his existential system of thought are the following principles:

    i.   That existence precedes essence.

    ii.   That it is up to the individual to choose the life they think best – human freedom.

As far as Sartre is concerned, human nature cannot be defined in advance because it is not completely thought out in advance. Man exists first of all before his essence is evolved as he confronts himself, emerges in the world and defines himself afterwards. He formulates his notion that 'existence precedes essence' to convey the idea that man exists first without a defined purpose; only finding himself in the world. Only then does man define himself as a reaction to the experience of just finding himself in the world. He argues that if man were an artifact, his essence would have come before his existence, and therefore, determines his nature. Unfortunately, man is not an artifact, he was created without a purpose, and therefore, he has no fixed nature. His nature is determined by his own choice; the way he exists and acts express his essence; that is, what we mean by man. Therefore, the essence of man is in his existence.

Aristotle has presented an argument in his *Ethics*, that man is created by God to fulfil some purpose. According to him, man finds fulfilment in life when he strives towards the purpose for which he is created. Flipping this argument, Sartre argues that since there is no God who designs man with a given purpose, the onus falls on the individual to choose the life he thinks best.

---

[70] . P. Stokes, p. 278.

Sartre's notion that 'existence precedes essence' implies that man has a greater dignity than stones or other beings. This greater dignity is a result of the fact that he consciously moves himself towards a future. In his contrast of man with other beings, he talks of two modes of being; being-in-itself and being-for-itself. Being-in-itself is the mode in which you find other beings, while man as a conscious subject exists as being-for-itself.

The consequence of the notion, that 'existence precedes essence', is not only expressed by the fact that man creates himself, but also lies in the fact man is responsible for his own existence as an individual. Other beings, like stones, for instance, cannot take such responsibility for themselves. And if it is the case that man's essential nature is already fixed, he cannot take responsibility for what he is. [71] Concerning human freedom, Sartre conceives of human freedom in terms of negation, annihilation and nothingness. Freedom for him is the capacity for negation and nihilation, which characterizes the being-for-itself. Freedom is built on the foundation of nothingness and negation provides the grounds for the possibility of questions. This implies that we can only ask questions because of the possibility of negation. The same possibility of negation makes imagination, especially that of a situation different from the existing one, possible.

In the opinion of Sartre, since man can asks questions, it means he is not subject to the universal causal order, for to be able to question it implies the ability to negate it. The power to negate is identical with freedom and it is rooted in the nothingness within man. This nothingness which man carries within himself is the foundation of his freedom. It is this same nothingness that makes man the kind of being that he is, namely, a being without support, a being impossible to identify with anything in a fixed or permanent way, a being that is not what he is and is what he is not. [72] By implication therefore, freedom is not just a quality of man, but man is freedom, for freedom is identical with his being.

The freedom of man goes with a heavy and inescapable responsibility and a disturbing anguish. That man is responsible for everything he does means that he cannot excuse himself or defer

---

[71] . B. Agidigbi, pp. 44-45.
[72] . Ibid., p. 46.

responsibility to a divine being or even human nature. If he does so, he is involved in self-deception or 'bad-faith'. Man may not be responsible for a situation beyond his control that he finds himself; he is nonetheless responsible for the way he reacts to that situation. Freedom and responsibility go together; to be free is to be responsible. Along with freedom too is the inevitability of choice, since to be free is to be compelled to choose. A free being cannot but choose; refusal to choose is actually a choice not to choose.

Sartre argues that man's awareness of the nature of his freedom and the responsibility that goes with the freedom grips him with anguish. As a matter of fact, it leads to three related burdens on him; anguish, abandonment, and despair. The anguish arises from his awareness of the weight of the responsibility his freedom places upon him. The abandonment arises from the knowledge of the fact that God does not exist, therefore, man is left alone, without guidance in matters of morals. Man has to make it up as he goes along. Lastly, despair arises from the fact that man acts without hope, because he cannot trust that things will turn out for the best. This is because there is no providence to rely on, except man's own will and action.

Self-deception or 'bad-faith', according to Sartre, is expressed in different forms. For instance:

i.   Belief in determinism

This is a denial of human freedom which some people take to, because of the fear of the reality of human freedom; they invent a theory of determinism. They start talking about human nature as the way in which they have been made by God and attribute what they do to human nature. Belief in human nature is a form of determinism.[73]

ii.   Spirit of Seriousness

This is another attitude of self-deception. According to Sartre absolute values, rights, and wrongs, are inscribed in nature and given to man *a priori*. In the view of Sartre, those who uphold this are

---

[73] . J. I. Omoregbe, p. 97.

cowards who think they have been freed from the anguish and responsibility of making personal choices and decisions.

iii.   Conformity to Social Moulds

This is the attitude of keeping to certain behavioural pattern so as to conform to social moulds. It is an impersonal way of life which Heidegger refers to as the "inauthentic life" and Sartre calls "bad-faith."

iv.   Avoiding or Postponing Decisions

This attitude plays itself out when, in the face of serious situations that demand immediate decisions, we postpone or avoid making decisions because we are afraid or uncomfortable with the unpleasant consequences of our decision. We pretend that things are not what we think they are. According to Sartre, it is self-deception. We live under the illusion that by postponing the decision, we have avoided making a decision, but the fact is, postponing the decision is itself a decision that we have made.

A striking aspect of Sartre's system of thought or existentialism is his atheism. He argues that man is created without essence or nature and thrown out there in the world without purpose. Therefore, he has to work out his essence and create a purpose for himself. This gives support to his view that 'existence precedes essence.' Sartre's novel, *Nausea* (1937), was in some ways a manifesto of atheistic existentialism. In the novel, he talks about the dejected researcher, Anthoine Roquentin, who became conscious of the fact that nature and every inanimate object are indifferent towards him and his tormented existence. They are extraneous to any human meaning and no human can see anything significant in them.[74] His lecture, "Existentialism and Humanism", which is sometimes referred to as "Existentialism is Humanism", outlines the fact that man makes himself, and therefore, rules out the role of God in human existence and all such things he referred to as "deterministic excuses".

---

[74] "Atheistic Existentialism" in www.en.wikipedia.org/wiki/Atheist_existentialism (Retrieved on 1/4/13).

There is no doubt that Sartre's existentialism is riddled with unavoidable burdens, for instance, that we are condemned to be free. Critics of his existentialism have accused him of pessimism. But according to Sartre, this is not the case, as existentialism exhibits optimism in the sense that the destiny of man is in his hands, and therefore, he should fashion it to realize his fulfilment.

Albert Camus (1913-1960)

Albert Camus is a celebrated French-Algerian author and great friend of Jean-Paul Sartre. He acquired popularity with his works, *The Stranger, The Outsider*, and *The Plague*. His great contribution to existentialism is contained in his, *The Myth of Sisyphus*.

In this work, *The Myth of Sisyphus*, he develops the existentialist theme of 'absurdity.' He argues that human existence is absurd, because humans try to make sense from a senseless world. The world is unreasonably silent about the needs of man; absurdity is a result of the confrontation between human need and the unreasonable silence of the world. With reference to the fate, Sisyphus was a man condemned by the gods to eternally push a boulder up the hill. The boulder ends up rolling down as soon as he reaches the top of the hill. Sisyphus will have to begin the push all over again.

According to Camus, the fate of Sisyphus describes the hopelessness and futility of human labour. Like Sisyphus, man lives his life without accomplishing anything. In the face of this, man's existence is pointless, and so, Camus asks, why should man not commit suicide? Camus argues that this is the inevitable conclusion of existentialism, which existentialists before him are afraid to say. He opines that existentialist thinkers and writers before him, failed to be faithful to the original premise of their existentialist philosophy; namely, that absurdity is the consequence of the confrontation between the irrational world and human rationality.

Camus argues further that there is no need to try to resolve this conflict between human rationality and an irrational world since; in the first place, it cannot be resolved. It is a given of human existence. Any attempt to resolve it is tantamount to denying the very phenomenon one began with. The very idea of suicide is an idea directed at resolving this conflict. According to Stokes,

Undoubtedly Camus backs himself, and his reader, into an inescapable corner. To accept absurdity is to accept death. To refuse it is to accept life on the precipice, with no leap to comfort, but only to live 'on the dizzying crest – that is integrity, the rest subterfuge.'[75]

By 'dizzying crest' Camus refers to the conscious experience of being alive in the face of death and pointless human toils, like Sisyphus in the face of serving his condemnation by the gods. According to Camus, 'revolt' is the appropriate action to be taken in the face of absurdity. 'Revolt' consists in being aware of our crushing fate and refusal to resign to it. Using Sisyphus' experience, he describes a situation where we are aware of the senselessness of our labour but not allowing it to despair our existence. For Sisyphus was fully aware of his condemnation to eternal repetition, but all the same, finds the lucidity that constitutes his torture as the same that crowns his victory. On the basis of this, he rejects suicide as an option to absurdity, for as he argues, we cannot solve the problem of absurdity by negating its existence. Absurdity is a necessary condition of the conflict between man and the world. To resort to suicide as a response to absurdity is to give in to defeat and to deny the very condition of human existence.

---

[75] . P. Stokes, p. 283.

PART TWO

PHENOMENOLOGY

Chapter

4

What Is Phenomenology?

Introduction

As a philosophical method, phenomenology is traced to the profound and creative criticism of British empiricism, which has its roots in Franz Brentano and Edmund Husserl in the later part of the 19th Century. They were not the only critics of British empiricism. Many other thinkers of different extractions, both in terms of backgrounds and traditions, were part and parcel of the criticism. Notable among them was the American philosopher, William James, whose original work in psychology influenced Husserl greatly.

Phenomenology can either be understood as a discipline in philosophy or as a movement in the history of philosophy. Here we are going to understand it not as a philosophical doctrine but a philosophical method, which means, it is a movement in the history of philosophy. The term phenomenology is derived from the word 'phenomenon' which means things, events or occurrences. Etymologically, phenomenology is derived from the two Greek words; 'phenomenon' as meaning 'appearance' and '*logos*' as meaning 'reason' or 'word.' Therefore, it means "reasoned inquiry"[76] As 'reasoned inquiry' it discovers the essences of appearances. By appearances, we refer to that which a person is conscious of. It is "the study of the structures of consciousness as experienced from the first-

---

[76] . D. Stewart and A. Mickunas (1974). *Exploring Phenomenology: A Guide to the Field and Its Literature*, USA: American Library Association, p. 3.

person point of view."[77] Basically, it is a study of the structure of the various types of experiences we have. These experiences range from perception, thought, memory, imagination, emotion, desire, and volition to our bodily awareness, embodied action, and social activity, even including linguistic activity. It "utilizes a distinctive method to study the structural features of experience and of things as experienced."[78] It is primarily a descriptive method that is undertaken in a way that is largely independent of scientific and causal explanations and accounts of the nature of experience. According to Kolawole Owolabi, it is a descriptive way by which we study phenomenon in its pure state, not allowing our preconceptions to interfere in our process of interpretation of what is.[79] The descriptive technique is very essential to the method of phenomenology.

This part of our text discusses the notion of phenomenology. It gives a conceptual analysis of the term and tries to outline the goals of phenomenology. It further discusses the notion of phenomenology within the context of its most renowned advocate, in the person of Edmund Husserl and finally abstracts the main themes of phenomenology for brief discussion.

The Concept of Phenomenology

Phenomenology as a philosophical method was almost exclusively used to refer to the method and movement that originated in the work of Edmund Husserl. There are, however, other prominent names that are associated with this method, for instance, Martin Heidegger, Maurice Merleau-Ponty, and Jean-Paul Sartre. The work of Husserl was an attempt to describe the experiences we have directly as we have them. He attempted to separate our experiences from their origins and development, separating them from the causal explanations that historians, sociologists or psychologists give to

---

[77] . D. W. Smith, "Phenomenology", *The Stanford Encyclopedia of Philosophy* (Fall 2011 Edition), Edward N. Zalta (ed.), URL=<http://plato.stanford.edu /achives/fall2011/entries/phenomenology/>
[78] "Phenomenology" in the *Internet Encyclopedia of Philosophy*, www.iep.utm.edu/ phenom/ (Retrieved on 8/3/13).
[79] . K. Owolabi[A] (1998). "The Phenomenological Movement" in A. Fadahunsi, (ed.), *Philosophy: An Anthology*, Lagos: ARK Publishers, p. 280.

them.[80] He rejected the Kantian dichotomy between what appears (phenomenon) and what is true or real (noumenon). Husserl does not agree with Kant on the noumenon. For him, all that exists is the phenomenon. He argues that philosophers should concern themselves with what appears immediately to consciousness. They should try to give an exact and careful description of what appears immediately to consciousness, since the truth lies in what appears and not what is behind it.[81]

After Husserl, the likes of Heidegger, Sartre and Merleau-Ponty refined the phenomenological method. Their reformation did not necessarily agree with the conclusions of Husserl.

Before Husserl, the term phenomenology had been used by Franz Brentano, Ernst Mach, and Alexander Pfander to describe or analyze phenomena. They used it to describe inquiries that look beyond what is directly given to us in our experiences. Hegel too, in his *Phenomenology of Spirit*, (1807) had used the term to describe how the spirit gradually makes its appearance. It is a process that begins with initial oppositions between itself that is the spirit and something else; between different forms of consciousness, and finally ending when all the separation is overcome with self-knowledge. This is what Hegel called the absolute knowledge.[82] The very first usage of phenomenology is however, traced to Johann Heinrich Lambert's *The New Organon* (1764). Here it describes the inquiry into our sensory experience, a theory of how things appear to us, how they seem to be.[83]

Tracing its usage, Simon Blackburn writes:

> A term that emerged in the 18th century, in the writings of Johann Heinrich Lambert ... and Kant, to denote the description of consciousness and experience in abstraction from consideration of its intentional content.... In Hegel, phenomenology is instead the historical enquiry into the evolution of self-consciousness, developing from elementary

---

[80] . R. Solomon (2000). "Phenomenology" in T. Mautner, (ed.), *The Penguin Dictionary of Philosophy*, London: Penguin Books, p. 421.

[81] . B. Agidigbi, p. 10.

[82] . R. Solomon, "Phenomenology".

[83] . Ibid.

sense experience to fully rational, free, thought processes
capable of yielding knowledge. The term in the 20th century
is associated with the work and school of Husserl.[84]

Concerning how we define phenomenology, Jim Unah writes that
"phenomenology derives from the word 'phenomena' or
'phenomenon,' which has crystallized into a technical philosophical
concept of diverse usage since the inception of Western
scholarship." [85] The word 'phenomena' refers to things, events or
occurrences.

Various philosophers use it in various ways. Some of such usages
include: Heidegger's use of it to refer to the totality of what is open
to us for inspection or that which can be brought to light. Lambert
uses it to describe the features of human experience that are illusory.
Therefore, for him, phenomenology will be the theory of illusion.
Kant uses phenomena to describe things as they appear to us as
distinct from things as they are in themselves. So, Kant will
understand phenomenology as the theory of things as they appear to
us. For Hegel, phenomena is the self-manifestations of universal
reason, therefore, phenomenology will be, for him, the science of the
self-actualization of the spirit as it moves from self-rejection to self-
reconciliation. Peirce understood phenomena as including all
observable entities and everything that can be constructed by the
mind. Therefore, phenomenology will be, for him, the study of
perceptions of objects or things; real or imagined.[86]

These various understandings of phenomena and the
corresponding understanding of phenomenology derived from them
indicate that there is a dichotomy between what appears to us and
what truly is. This implies that things have a double which are not
open to our normal ordinary perceptual abilities. Therefore, Unah
describes phenomenology as "the study of the transient, ephemeral,
outward features of human experience."[87]

---

[84] . S. Blackburn, pp. 284-285.
[85] . J. I. Unah (1996). "Phenomenology" in J. I. Unah, (ed.), *Metaphysics, Phenomenology and African Philosophy*, Ibadan: Hope Publications, p. 205.
[86] . Ibid., pp. 205-206.
[87] . Ibid., p. 206.

For Husserl, to whom the concept of phenomenology has been closely related in Contemporary Western philosophy, 'phenomena' describe objects the way they are experienced by the transcendental self. Objects manifest themselves or appear as they are. The way we perceive them is not determined by the way they appear or manifest themselves but by the way and manner we position ourselves in relation to them. Therefore, if there is a distortion of reality, it is not in the manifestation or appearance of the object of perception but in the way and manner we are positioned in perceiving them.

> If we approach objects and events from a position of bias, prejudice, pre-conception or predisposition we end up with a grotesque and distorted picture of such objects and events. But if we approach things from a predispositionless, unbiased, unprejudiced, position we easily understand things as they are for we are thus enabled to grasp their essences.[88]

The implication of this is that in the opinion of phenomenologists, phenomena as things and events are capable of being known just as they are. It means that things and events do not appear to us different from what they truly are, neither do they hide aspects of themselves when they manifest themselves. Therefore, they are capable of being known as they are. If we do not know them as they are, it is because of our predispositions and preconceptions that we cannot grasp their essences.

Some Definitions of Phenomenology

According to Anthony Okeregbe, any attempt to define phenomenology leaves one intellectually entrapped in a web of lexical and conceptual confusion.[89] This submission notwithstanding, scholars have made some attempts to define the concept of phenomenology. For instance, in Gregory Pence's *A Dictionary of Common Philosophical Terms*, phenomenology is defined as "a non-homogeneous, twentieth-century philosophical movement associated

---

[88] . Ibid., p. 207.
[89] . A. O. Okeregbe, (1996), "Phenomenology as Metaphysics" in J. I. Unah (ed.), p. 243.

with but not limited to Husserl. It is, most simply, the analysis of consciousness, the nature of essences as perceived in consciousness, and the nature of human experience independent of cause and psychological explanation."[90]This definition puts together the general concerns of the phenomenological method as they appear in the works of Husserl. However, it serves the purpose of giving us an idea of what the central concerns and themes of phenomenology are.

Maurice Natanson, who is very consistent with Husserlian phenomenology, explains phenomenology "as a mysticism whose central concern is a dark realm of essences, as an intuitionism of a Bergsonian order, as an anti-scientific doctrine, or as a philosophy that denies the reality of the world by bracketing out existence."[91] This means that phenomenology, as a concept, describes the philosophical movement whose primary objective is to directly investigate and describe phenomenon as it is consciously experienced. There are no theories about their causal explanation, nor are they trapped in unexamined preconceptions and presuppositions.

For phenomenologists, objects always reveal their true states if allowed to do so because phenomena are in their exact positions, only our prejudices disallow us from perceiving them correctly. Phenomenologists conceive the Kantian distinction between the *noumena* (things as they are) and the *phenomena* (things as they appear to us), as a misnomer. The polarity Kant suggests in this distinction is only possible because we fail to allow things as they are to reveal themselves to us. As far as phenomenologists are concerned, the noumenon is in the phenomenon. Thus, Merleau-Ponty defines phenomenology as:

> A transcendental philosophy which places in abeyance the assertions arising out of the natural attitude, it is also a philosophy for which the world is always "already there" before reflection begins – as an inalienable presence and all its efforts are concentrated upon reaching a direct and primitive contact

[90] . G. Pence (2000). *A Dictionary of Common Philosophical Terms*, New York: McGrawHill Companies Ltd., p. 42.
[91] . M. Natanson (1968). *Literature, Philosophy and the Social Sciences: Existentialism and Phenomenology*. Hague: MartinusNijhoff, p. 5.

with the world and ending that contact with a philosophical status. It is the search for a philosophy which shall be a rigorous science. It tries to give a direct description of our experience as it is without taking account of its psychological origin.[92]

According to Omoregbe, "phenomenology is a method of philosophizing, a philosophical method which aims at an unprejudiced description of the objects of experience."[93] Oyeshile refers to it as "the descriptive study of phenomena, of thought, in their pure and unadulterated form without our prejudices influencing our description."[94] It is a position in which we intuit and describe things as they appear to us directly or immediately before we begin to reflect on or interpret what we have experienced. This implies that the aim of phenomenology is to perceive the object of inquiry with a completely open mind, without any presuppositions, bias or prior assumptions. This is to be done by putting between brackets or suspending all prior assumptions and suppositions and conceptions of the object of inquiry so that the mind becomes free and open to receive the object of experience just the way it appears to the consciousness of the perceiver in experience.[95]

It is a presuppositionless description of the given facts of experience. It operates on the basis that if the subject of inquiry approaches the object of inquiry from a position of bias, prejudice, preconception or predisposition, the subject ends up with a distorted view of the object. If on the contrary the reverse is the case, then the subject can easily understand the object as it is, because he grasps the essence of the object. In other words, what leads to distortion of reality is not the way things appear but the way and manner we position ourselves in relation to them. That is to say, the way and manner we observe and comprehend them.

---

[92] . M. Merleau-Ponty (1962). *The Phenomenology of Perception*, trans. by Coline Smith, New York: The Humanities Press, p. viii.

[93] . J. Omoregbe (2001). *Philosophy of Mind: An Introduction to Philosophical Psychology*. Lagos: Joja Educational Research and Publishers Limited, p. 21.

[94] O. Oyeshile (2006). "An Existentialist Critique of Husserlian Phenomenological Approach to Knowledge" in R. A. Akanmidu (ed.), *Footprints in Philosophy*, Ibadan: Hope Publications, p. 45.

[95] . J. Omoregbe, p. 21.

This way of perceiving the object, that is, the phenomenological way, is referred to as an 'eidetic reduction.' It means the perceiver removes from the object of perception "all existential traits, all its peculiar characteristics and all its accidental qualities so that only its essence is left."[96] What the phenomenologist is looking for is the essence of things. He is not interested in the particular qualities or existential traits of things. Therefore, Husserl describes phenomenology as an 'eidetic science', that is, the science of essences.

Phenomenology can be said to be the *logos* of the phenomenon. By *logos*, we mean "an utterance, an account, a discourse, a thought, a reason why, the faculty of reason, etc."[97] And by 'phenomenon' we mean "a thing (a quality, a relation, a state of affairs, an event, etc) as it appears to us, as it is perceived."[98] For Husserl, 'phenomenon' refers to that which manifests itself directly through the acts of consciousness. This is in contrast to the idea of the phenomenon as an empirical manifestation in opposition to the 'noumenon,' as we find in Kant. As the *logos* of the phenomenon, phenomenology deals with the descriptive explanation of what presents itself to our consciousness, as it presents itself to our consciousness, in so far as it presents itself to our consciousness. In logical language, this will be the equivalent of the "if and only if" situation.

The operative theme here is 'consciousness' hence Natanson argues that to truly understand the meaning of phenomenology, we need to enquire into the intentionality of consciousness. Therefore, phenomenology can be understood as "an epistemologically neutral instrument for the inspection of the presentation of consciousness."[99] Husserl, in agreement with Brentano, "realized that intentionality was the distinctive mark of consciousness, and saw in it a concept capable of overcoming traditional mind-body dualism." [100] He, Husserl, rejects the dualism of the mind and the body. We shall discuss his idea of consciousness below in chapters five and six.

---

[96] . Ibid., p. 22.
[97] . T. Mautner (ed.) (2000). *"logos"* in *The Penguin Dictionary of Philosophy*, London: Penguin Books, p. 327.
[98] . Ibid. "Phenomenon", p. 421.
[99] . M. Natanson, p. 10.
[100] S. Blackburn, p. 285.

According to James Edie,

Phenomenology is neither a science of objects nor a science of the subject; it is a science of *experience*. It does not concentrate exclusively on either the objects of experience or on the subject of experience, but on the point of contact where being and consciousness meet. It is therefore, a study of consciousness *as intentional*, as directed towards objects, as living in an intentionally constituted world.[101]

This understanding of phenomenology clearly shows that the object (*noema*) and the subject (*noesis*) are not studied independently of each other but in their correlativity on each level of experience. The levels of experience include perception, imagination, categorical thought, etc. A study of this nature seeks to disclose the structures of consciousness as consciousness, and of experience as experience. It is a study that enquires into the fundamental structures of conscious experience; that is, the structures that constitute the conditions of the possibility of our conscious experience whatsoever.[102] Within this context, we can conveniently refer to phenomenology as "radical empiricism" whose concern is with the fullness of experience in its concrete, total, and existential density.

According to Pierre Thevenaz, "phenomenology seems to be a *Proteus* which appears now as an objective inquiry into the logic of essences and meanings, now as a theory of abstraction, now as a deep psychological description or analysis of consciousness, now as speculation on the 'transcendental Ego,' now as a method for approaching concretely lived existence, and finally, as in Sartre and Merleau-Ponty, seems to blend purely with existentialism."[103] The suggestion here is that, there are many sides to phenomenology. As a method of philosophical enquiry, it approaches the object of inquiry from different directions and perspectives. The primary aim, however, is to comprehend the essence of the object of study. Therefore, the interest of Husserl in phenomenology is logic and epistemology.

---

[101] .J. M. Edie (1962). "Introduction" in Pierre Thevenaz, *What is Phenomenology? And Other Essays* edited by J. M. Edie, Chicago: Quadrangle Books, p. 19.

[102] Ibid, p. 20.

[103] .P. Thevenaz (1962). *What is Phenomenology? And Other Essays* edited by J. M. Edie, Chicago: Quadrangle Books, p. 37.

Nonetheless, we must admit that in the process, he laid the foundations for a revolutionary metaphysics of experience.

Although phenomenologists argue that things and events can be known exactly as they are, since objects of experience show themselves as they are. This notwithstanding, they claim that to perceive things as they are, is not the right of every subject. Rather, it is the exclusive preserve of a purified and detached ego. The purified and detached ego is the presuppositionless mind.

The Goals of Phenomenology

According to Oyeshile, "the diversity of points of view held by philosophers working within the phenomenological tradition not only makes the summary of the phenomenological tenets difficult, it also points out the fact that other descriptions of phenomenology with regards to different areas are possible."[104] The work of David Stewart and Algis Mickunas, however, gives an insight into what the basic tenets of phenomenology are. For them, it is "a return to the traditional tasks of philosophy without presuppositions, the intentionality of consciousness and the refusal of the subject-object dichotomy."[105] Therefore, the basic objective of phenomenology is to analyze human experience such that the subject of inquiry is able to grasp the object of inquiry in its pure state. Therefore, it is to be understood as a philosophy of creative intuition.[106]

There is no recognizable consensus among phenomenologists about the direction of the phenomenological method. For instance, Husserl conceives it as an epistemological project. His aim was to develop the phenomenological method as a paradigm of philosophy, with the overall objective of re-establishing philosophy as the foundation of all disciplines. He thinks, with this method, he will provide an epistemic foundation in the Cartesian spirit. He will succeed to purge philosophy of predilections and make it a purely scientific enterprise that will be capable of supporting other disciplines, and at the same time, establish an indubitable foundation of cognition. This will serve as the ultimate foundation of all other

---

[104] O. Oyeshile, p. 44.
[105] .D. Stewart and A. Mickunas, p. 4.
[106] .O. Oyeshile, p. 45.

beliefs. [107] Some other phenomenologists, however, consider it a metaphysical project necessary for the proper understanding of ontology.

Okeregbe expands the goals of phenomenology when he lucidly itemized and outlined the following as the goals of phenomenology:

i.   It seeks to find and develop itself as a presuppositionless philosophy.

ii. It seeks a 'return to the things themselves' of immediate experience.

iii. It seeks to clarify the meanings of the fundamental terms, basic concepts, and essential categories of all special or higher level disciplines, including the natural sciences.

iv. It seeks to locate and clarify the *a priori* structure of all so-called regional ontologies.

v.   It seeks to return to the Cartesian and Leibnizian ideal of a *mathesis universalis* while at the same time it tries to reconstruct its character with regard to a point of departure and an ultimate goal for a fully realized science of man. vi. It seeks to continue the essential style of transcendental philosophy involved in Kant's *Critique of Pure Reason* while at the same time critiques Kant's transcendental philosophy as a further development of Kantianism.

vi. It seeks to reconstruct the total range of the life of consciousness in terms of its underlying eidetic structure from the standpoint of transcendental subjectivity. viii. It seeks to understand the genesis of meaning in nature and in history and endeavors to describe the sedimentation of meaning that lie within the evolution of our experience.

vii. It seeks to reconstruct the life-world within which each one is formed, exists and dies. [108]

These goals are mutually related and together give an insight into the overall theses of phenomenology. They therefore, expose the grounding principles of Husserlian thought, namely:

---

[107] .K. Owolabi,[A] p. 281.
[108] . A. O. Okeregbe, p. 245.

    i.   Phenomenology presents a unique method of pursuing its special ends by developing a theory of *epoche* and of reductions.

    ii.   Phenomenology presents a radical theory of consciousness and that of intentionality.

    iii.   Phenomenology expresses a new theory of meaning that is intimately bound with the Husserlian theory of essence. iv. Phenomenology requires and presents a special theory of evidence developed in terms of 'self-evidence.'

    iv.   Phenomenology articulates a theory of transcendental consciousness in which the constitutive activity of the transcendental ego emerges as the sovereign theme.[109]

---

[109] Ibid., p. 246.

Chapter

5

Husserlian Phenomenology

Introduction

Although the term 'phenomenology' preceded Husserl, it was only under the leadership of Husserl that it became a philosophical method before the First World War. Edmund Husserl (1859-1938) was a mathematician, who became a philosopher. As a philosopher, he was concerned with the search for what he called 'the Archimedean point' of philosophy; that is, the foundation of human knowledge. He believed that this can be found or arrived at by detaching oneself from views and beliefs that were previously held, that is, by bracketing off one's biases, prejudices and predilections.[110] The primary aim of Husserl was to discern the essential nature of mental acts and thereby arrive at the truths that constitute the sources of human knowledge.

Husserl's efforts and the eventual evolution of the phenomenological method are situated within the framework of eliminating skepticism and creating an indubitable foundation for knowledge. The threat of skepticism has always prompted the need to firmly establish the foundations of knowledge in modern Western philosophy, especially after the skepticism of the 16th Century attacked virtually everything, undermining and nearly crippling all the efforts in academics, politics, religion, and the spiritual unity of Europe. Skepticism called to question the certainty of science and

---

[110] .O. Oyeshile, p. 40.

faith.[111] From Descartes to Brentano, philosophers made concerted efforts to ground human knowledge.

Background to Husserlian Thought

Husserl begins his philosophy from the natural standpoint of our everyday world as we experience it. He adopted the method that is now called 'phenomenological reduction' in which we "ignore all previously held personal, philosophical, and even scientific assumptions associated with a thing and then examine what remains."[112] The idea of this reduction is to unravel how the mind works. Husserl believed that this reduction can be retro-activated on consciousness itself in order to attain apodictic certainty.

Husserl owes his interest and development of the phenomenological method to Brentano's interest in the concept of 'intentionality' and the descriptive investigation of inner perceptions.[113] According to Husserl, he got to understand through Brentano's psychological theory of the mind that philosophy could be a rigorous science. Brentano's psychological theory of the mind, which was developed under the Aristotelian, Scholastic and Cartesian influences, was itself centered on the concept of intentionality. The theory argues that "the mind is differentiated from physical reality by its ability to intend or refer to something beyond itself."[114] In the opinion of Husserl, philosophy had abandoned the task of becoming a strict science, which means that it has lost its sense of direction. Philosophy should be a rigorous science; it should investigate the most radical, fundamental, primitive, original evidences of conscious experience. This means that philosophy goes beneath the constructions of science and commonsense and investigates the foundations of these constructions in experience. As Edie puts it:

---

[111] .Ibid., p. 41.

[112] . J. Weate (ed.) (1998). *A Young Person's Guide to Philosophy*, London: Dorling Kindersley, p. 60.

[113] . O. Oyeshile, p. 47 where he quotes M. Farber, (1943), *The Foundation of Phenomenology*, Albany: State University of New York Press, p. 8.

[114] . B. A. G. Fuller (1966). *A History of Philosophy*, 3rd Ed., New York: Holt, Rinehart and Winston, p. 550.

It studies what all the particular sciences take for granted and what we in "natural" everyday experience take for granted. A "presuppositionless" philosophy is one which will reach what is absolutely primary or most fundamental in experience.[115]

According to Husserl, after Plato and Aristotle, subsequent philosophers neglected the rigorous aspect of philosophy and thus, philosophy became chaotic. This was the consequence of the tendency to view philosophy through the mirror of the natural sciences because of the successes that the natural sciences have recorded. According to Husserl, this tendency which he described as 'naturalistic objectivism' is the triumph of naturalism and the collapse of rationalism. For Husserl, philosophy will regain its lost status if it becomes phenomenological.[116]

Husserl and the Method of Phenomenology

In an attempt to deconstruct modern Western philosophy, Husserl argued in his *Philosophy and the Crisis of European Man* (1936) that Western culture lost its true direction and purpose when philosophy departed from its original goal. The original goal of philosophy was "to provide answers for the human and humane concerns of humanity by dealing vigorously with the human quest for the highest values, which consist in developing the unique broad range capacities of human reason."[117] There was a collapse of rationalism, in his opinion, and he set for himself the task of saving human reason. That which human reason is to be saved from provides the background for his phenomenology. He, therefore, attempts to develop a proper method through which we can grasp the essential nature of things in order to overcome the naturalistic objectivism of the natural sciences that is eroding rationalism. His attempt led to the formulation of the two parts of his phenomenology, namely, (i) descriptive phenomenology and (ii) transcendental phenomenology.

---

[115] J. M. Edie, pp. 18-19.
[116] O. Oyeshile, p. 47.
[117] Ibid.

Descriptive Phenomenology

This aspect of Husserlian phenomenology reflects the great influence of Brentano on him. It concerns itself with the descriptive analysis of human experience just as it occurs. Meaning that it leaves out from this analysis any prejudices and prior assumptions or presuppositions. This is aimed at achieving an objective, unbiased knowledge. Phenomenology, at this stage, is not concerned with the existential aspects of things. It is rather interested in the essence of things. And Husserl arrives at this essence through his method of *epoche*, which is the same as 'eidetic reduction' or 'science of essences'.

The method of *epoche* consists in bracketing the existential aspects of things so as to intuit their essences. It is a detachment from any form of biases, emotions, prejudices, presuppositions, and preconceptions, so as to contemplate the essence of phenomena.

Husserl refers to phenomenology as 20th Century Cartesianism and credits Descartes as the genuine patriarch of phenomenology, because it was Descartes who prompted his quest for the foundation of knowledge. Like Descartes, he starts from the thinking self.[118] It, therefore, means that the Cartesian 'radical doubt' is the predecessor of the phenomenological method. Although, Husserl and Descartes share the same starting point, there are, however, basic differences in their methods. While Descartes seeks to arrive at certain knowledge through systematic doubt, Husserl opines that we must decide to disregard all our present knowledge including the presupposition that we must arrive at an absolute foundation of knowledge as is the case in the systematic doubt of Descartes. Therefore, Husserl takes a more radical approach than Descartes does. He chooses to look at things and facts themselves as they are given in actual experience and intuition; he judges only by evidence. As Stumpf puts it, "Husserl simply withheld any judgment about experiences, seeking instead to describe his experiences as fully as possible in terms of the evidence of experience itself."[119]

For both Descartes and Husserl, experience revolves around the self, the ego, and the ego is the source of all knowledge. While for

---

[118] S.E. Stumpf (1988), p. 488.
[119] Ibid.

Descartes, the ego is the first axiom in a logical sequence that eventually leads him to knowledge of reality, Husserl sees the ego as simply the matrix of experience, and therefore, puts the primary emphasis on experience rather than on logic. His primary concern is to discover and describe that which is given in experience, just as it is presented in its pure form.

Husserl criticized Descartes for going beyond the ego to the notion of extended substance, body, which ties the subject to an objective reality, and thereby producing the mind-body dualism. For Husserl, "pure subjectivity more accurately describes the actual facts of experience."[120] Rather than the *ergo cogito* (I think) of Descartes, Husserl argues that the *ergo cogito cogitatum* (I think something) more accurately describes experience as it is the typical human experience. Oyeshile summarizes Husserl's repudiation of Descartes thus:

> The significance of Husserl's repudiation of Descartes is that there is always a link between consciousness and thinking which is identified in the object of thought and the element of intentionality that creates the phenomena of experience. Husserl's emphasis that there is an indissoluble intentionality is a direct influence of his teacher, Brentano, who insisted that all psychological acts – thinking, desiring, linking, loving, hating and so forth – are object-oriented.[121]

It should be noted that Husserl did not only disagree with Descartes on the mind-body dualism, he also rejected the Kantian distinction between things as they are in themselves (noumenon) and things as they appear to us (phenomenon). He argues that the phenomenon is one and the same as the noumenon and only that which we see clearly and distinctly in internal experience is valid. Husserl rejected Kantian distinction because it implies that the essences of things do not appear to us, and therefore, cannot be known; whereas for Husserl, the objects of phenomenological knowledge are precisely the essences of things.[122]

---

[120] Ibid., p. 489.
[121] O. Oyeshile, p. 49.
[122] Ibid., pp. 49-50; quoting J. I. Omoregbe (1990). "Husserlian Phenomenology and Existential Phenomenology" in *The Nigerian Journal of Philosophy*, vol.10, Nos. 1 & 2, p. 16.

Transcendental Phenomenology

The purely descriptive phenomenology of Husserl gradually developed into transcendental idealism. According to Husserl, the ego discovers itself and it is in the being of the ego that the world consists. His argument is that, "as the ego increases its subjectivity, it becomes removed from the empirical realm and subsequently becomes a transcendental ego."[123] This becomes possible as a result of the double bracketing of the empirical world and the natural self of the subject. The bracketing of the natural self, that is referred to as 'transcendental reduction' gives way to the transcendental self.

Transcendental reduction is a process by which the subject reduces his natural self as well as his psychological life to the transcendental and phenomenological experience. By psychological life, we mean the domain of our internal psychological experience. The objective world, in its past, present, and future, is drawn from the self, therefore, all the existential meaning and value of the objective world is drawn from the transcendental self. It means then that the transcendental ego is no longer part of the empirical world, and in fact, the transcendental ego is responsible for the creation of the world. At this point, the transcendental ego is above the world and it can look back at itself as an ego that was previously immersed in the world. [124] Husserlian phenomenology, which spells out the basic teachings of phenomenological method, does not go without criticism. From the point of view of epistemology and ontology, Husserl underlines a very important idea, namely that the essences of phenomena are very vital to the understanding of reality. We can credit Husserl for lucidly pointing out that it is possible and indeed desirable to get to the essence of things through appearance. In this regard, his descriptive phenomenology is of immerse benefit.

The all important question, however, is whether it is possible to have a bias-free, 'presuppositionless' and 'preconceptionless' knowledge. Such knowledge is impossible and unrealistic. To be biasfree is to strip ourselves of all our existential characteristics. As long as we exist, we exist as existential beings and cannot but be

---

[123] .Ibid.
[124] .Ibid.

saddled with our existential characteristics or features. Husserl's advocacy for a bias-free understanding of the object is to guarantee objectivity. While we cannot downplay the value of objectivity, we, at the same time, cannot devoid ourselves of our existential features as being in existence; for to be in existence (being) is to be necessarily vested with existential characteristics.

The Phenomenological Method

The phenomenological method is a way of describing rather than a way of explaining. It stands in contradistinction to the scientific method. While the scientific method tries to go behind the data of experience to seek out the laws of nature that govern the behaviour of things and make them as they are, the phenomenological method tries to describe the elements within our environment as we experience them. The scientific method in an attempt to explain the laws of nature loses sight of the original data altogether. It does not acknowledge the human and existential reality of free decision making. It, therefore, assumes that the important data are those that fit its already preconceived criteria of significance.

To thoroughly understand the phenomenological method, we need to come to terms with two recurrent standpoints in Husserl's philosophy. These standpoints are the 'natural standpoint' and the 'phenomenological standpoint.' They are epistemological standpoints that confront any philosopher who seeks to attain understanding and meaning. They both correspond to the mode of operation employed by a natural attitude and a phenomenological attitude.[125] We will appreciate the phenomenological method when we transcend the natural attitude and employ the phenomenological attitude as the ontological foundation in evaluating knowledge. Therefore, the step one in understanding the phenomenological method is to understand the natural attitude.

The Natural Attitude

The natural attitude in the works of Husserl refers to the stage of pre-philosophical standpoint; this is, the attitude of everyday life. It

---

[125] A.O. Okeregbe, p. 246.

consists in the evaluation of experience according to the dictates of our superficial thinking. This is a thinking that is characterized and influenced by unexpected and uncontrollable happenings or changes of our everyday life. It is what epistemology will call naïve realism. It takes knowledge of the world and reality for granted. Husserl describes the natural attitude thus:

> I am aware of a world, spread out in space endlessly and in time becoming and without end. I am aware of it, that means first of all, I discover it immediately, intuitively, I experience it. Through sight, touch, hearing, etc. in the different ways of sensory perception, corporeal things, somehow spatially distributed are for me simply there.[126]

This description of the natural attitude implies that out there, there is a real external world, which exists in space and time and is much the same for all humans in relation to our daily experiences of this world. It also implies a blind acceptance of what the senses present to us about this external world as valid knowledge. The natural attitude is contented with the epistemological role of the passive and uncritical observation of the world. This is why doubts, fears and anxieties besiege our understanding at the level of natural attitude, since it takes the veracity of the data presented by the senses about the world for granted.

The Phenomenological Attitude

The phenomenological attitude on the contrary is a transcendental stage which Husserl refers to as the arithmetical world. At this stage we reflect on the ideas given by nature; we are purged and purified of what is given in and by the natural attitude. Husserl refers to the sciences of the natural attitude as dogmatic because they take for granted that which is conventional, which at in-depth reflection become problematic, while those of the phenomenological attitude are critical.

According to him,

---

[126] . E. Husserl[A] (1969). *Ideas: General Introduction to Pure Phenomenology*. Trans. W.R.Boyce Gibson. London: Allen and Unwin Ltd., p. 6.

On one side stand the sciences of the dogmatic standpoint, facing the facts misconceived about all problems of an epistemological or skeptical kind. They take their start from the primordial 'givenness' of the facts they deal with and they ask what the nature of the immediately given facts may be, and what can be immediately infused from that natural ground concerning these same facts and those of the domain as a whole. On the other side we have the rigorous inquiries of the epistemological, the especially philosophical standpoint.[127]

The implication of Husserl's statement is that, to the level at which the sciences of the natural standpoint have developed in exact sciences, we find them clear and comprehensible. Therefore, we get the impression that we have gotten the truth of reality, based on the reliable methods of objectivity. If, however, we decide to give a deeper and more reflective thought to what we have, we find errors and some confusion as we become entangled in patent difficulties and self-contradictions. We are faced with the danger of falling into skepticism.[128]

Owolabi interprets the Husserlian distinction between the natural and phenomenological attitudes as meaning that a genuine theory of knowledge cannot be grounded on the natural standpoint since that will impoverish the very essence of epistemology.[129] The very essence of epistemology is to critique theoretical reason. To do this, Husserl calls for the transcendence of the natural attitude to the phenomenological attitude so as to give knowledge a genuine epistemological foundation. In simple terms, it implies that genuine philosophy begins at the phenomenological stage. Therefore, Husserl invites us to put aside the natural standpoint and hold onto the phenomenological standpoint.

---

[127] .Ibid., p. 96.
[128] . E. Husserl[A] (1970). *The Idea of Phenomenology*, Trans. by William Alston and George Naknikian. The Hague: MartinusNijhoff, p. 17.
[129] . K. Owolabi[A] (1992). "The Dichotomy between the Natural Attitude and Phenomenological Attitude in the Philosophy of Edmund Husserl" in *The Nigerian Journal of Philosophy*, vol.12, nos.1 & 2. University of Lagos: Department of Philosophy, pp. 50-64.

The constant feature of Husserlian phenomenology is the idea of a rigorous science and this is why Husserl emphasizes the eidetic science; the science aimed at discovering the essence of things. He had criticized the sciences of the natural order arguing that they needed readjustments to overcome their superfluity. In his opinion, the superfluity is based on:

    i.   The degeneration of the sciences into an unphilosophical study of mere facts which has made science to lose the significance for man's life as a whole.

    ii.   Its [science] naturalistic attitude which has rendered science incapable of coping with the problem of absolute truth and validity.[130]

To achieve the rigor required by the phenomenological science, we have to be philosophically radical by turning to things or objects as the roots of the rigorous science. Further investigations, according to Husserl, show that beyond things or objects, there is something that lies deeper in the consciousness of the knowing subject to whom the things or objects are manifested. This is what he referred to as 'transcendental subjectivity.' This implies that you first 'turn to the object' and then 'turn to the subject'. It is in these turns that misunderstandings about the phenomenological method arise. In turning to the subject, according to Husserl, we will have to radically scrutinize the object. This consists in a methodological suspension of the general thesis which makes up the natural attitude. This is where Husserl introduces his popular phenomenological *epoche*. This is discussed in the next section as one of the key themes in phenomenology. At this point we need to outline the major themes and concepts which constitute the framework with which Husserlian phenomenology and the phenomenological method are built.

---

[130] A. O. Okeregbe, p. 250.

Chapter

6

Key Themes in Phenomenology

Introduction

Every philosophical system has its own basic themes and concepts that encompass its teaching and beliefs. Phenomenology is not an exception. The understanding of the key themes of phenomenology will certainly boost our understanding of the phenomenological method. The key themes are means by which phenomenologists seek to realize the objective of phenomenology as a descriptive and rigorous science. Here we shall discuss the two most central themes; *epoche* and intentionality.

Epoche

This can also be referred to as the 'method of reduction.' The term *epoche* is the Greek term for bracketing or suspension of belief. Husserl uses it to describe his method of phenomenological suspension in which we detach ourselves from any viewpoints with regards to the objective world. It means the removal from our minds all and any prejudices, prior beliefs, and assumptions concerning the object of investigation. This will enable us approach our investigation of the object with an open mind.[131]

The idea of *epoche* or phenomenological bracketing was introduced to phenomenology by Husserl. He borrowed it from mathematics. As a mathematical method, it is employed in resolving

---

[131] .J. Omoregbe (2001). *Philosophy of Mind,* p. 24.

interrelated or complex problems. It attends to complex problems in piece-meal manner without further complicating the problem. As employed by Husserl in phenomenology, it serves to put aside dubious and controversial cognition from the natural standpoint. Kostenbaun describes *epoche* as "the act of focusing on any part or all of my experience and then observing, analyzing, abstracting, and describing that experience by removing myself from the immediate and lived engagement in it."[132] Owolabi interprets this as "the process of sweeping off the prejudices of the natural standpoint in order to attain the phenomenological standpoint."[133]

Husserl himself describes what he means by *epoche* thus:

> The thesis undergoes a modification whilst remaining in itself what it is; we set it as it were "out of action." We "disconnect it", "bracket it." It still remains there like the bracketed in the bracket, like the disconnected outside the connexional system. The thesis is experienced as lived (*Erlebnis*) but we make no use of it, and by that, of course, we do not indicate privation as when we say of the ignorant that he makes no use of certain thesis[134]

The *epoche* extends to all phenomena and elements of experience, including people, things, beliefs, cultural situations, etc. To bracket all phenomena does not necessarily mean to put them off; it rather means that we look at them necessarily judging whether they are realities or appearances. We abstain from passing opinions or judgments, or valuations about them; it is standing back from things. It enables us to review the naivety that characterizes the natural attitude in the light of the phenomenological attitude. It helps us to destroy all interest so that we can rebuild our experience; it is the demolition exercise, according to Unah, which is motivated by the genuine desire to reconstruct. It gravitates us "towards the essential structures of experience or that we construct the world as it is when

---

[132] P. Kostenbaun, "Introductory Essay", *The Paris Lectures*, p. x.
[133] K. Owolabi,[A] p. 286.
[134] E. Husserl,[A] p. 108.

we suspend all judgments as we focus attention on the given fact of experience."[135] According to Husserl, *epoche* means that:

> We put out of action the general thesis which belongs to the essence of the natural standpoint, we place in brackets whatever it includes respecting the nature of being: this entire natural world therefore which is continually 'there for us', 'present to our hand' and will ever remain there, is a fact about the world of which we continue to be conscious, even though it pleases us to put it in brackets. If I do this, as I am fully free to do, I do not then deny this world as though I were a sophist, I do not doubt that it is there as though I were a skeptic; but I use the phenomenological *epoche* which completely bars me from using any judgment that concerns spatio-temporal existence.[136]

From Husserl's description, *epoche* is a way of putting aside all unnecessary data of experience, this will enable the perceiver to analyze and interpret a particular process of experience. It is a process of perception that encourages us to fully concentrate on the particular object or phenomenon of perception. It suspends all previous ideas about a given phenomenon of cognition so as to concentrate on the immediate and direct data of the phenomenon. It is simply correct to say that bracketing is an epistemological tool used to get the epistemic subject ready to obtain a perfect and immediate knowledge of phenomenon.[137]

It is important that we distinguish the Husserlian notion of *epoche* from the Cartesian idea of methodic doubt. While Husserl uses the notion of *epoche* to describe his detachment from any point of view concerning the objective world, Descartes uses the idea of methodic doubt to describe his refusal to believe and accept any proposition that he cannot perceive clearly and distinctly. Therefore, Descartes proceeded to doubt everything; all phenomena, including the world, except his thinking self. On the contrary, Husserl brackets all the elements of experience, refusing to assert that the world exists or not, he brackets the entire constitution of our experienced life; objects,

---

[135] .J. I. Unah, p. 217.
[136] .E.A. Husserl, pp. 110-111.
[137] .K.A. Owolabi, p. 287

other people, and cultural institutions. Husserlian bracketing simply means to abstain from asserting phenomena as real or appearance. In this *epoche*, Husserl discovers himself as the ego. By the ego, we mean the consciousness in which consists the objective world as it exists in its entirety. In contrast to this, is the fact that Descartes deduced the objective world from the residual certainty of the ego.[138]

Husserl's *epoche* is no doubt an epistemic method aimed at attaining immediate apodictic knowledge following the spirit of Descartes' methodic doubt. It is, however, not to be confused with the Cartesian method. In *epoche*, the epistemic subject is not in doubt about his previous beliefs like in the Cartesian methodic doubt. The epistemic subject only puts aside his previous ideas and suppositions, for the moment, about the object of cognition, to allow him have a prejudice-free cognition. This is not the same as doubting all previously held beliefs about the object of cognition, either sincerely or pretentiously, as it is the case in the Cartesian methodic doubt. It is a caution to the epistemic subject in his process of observation, not to becloud the phenomenon with his previously held beliefs, prejudices, suppositions, and biases.

For Husserl, therefore, the world is simply all that we are aware of and what appears valid to us in our actions of thought. Therefore, he argues that we should not assert anything about that which we do not see ourselves. By this very fact, he rejects the Cartesian and Kantian notions that reality goes beyond the immediate phenomenal realm. According to Husserl, the *epoche* enables us to discover the original, primordial, mode of experience. What we find here is consciousness and the objects of consciousness. The ego is the source of objects and what they mean because in the ego, we always find the irreducible element of experience. It means therefore, that objects appear as they

An Introduction to Existentialism, Phenomenology, and Hermeneutics
are determined by the structure of the ego or thinking self. That is to say, that "the meaning and being of things is primordially constituted in and through consciousness."[139] Husserl refers to this as the act of intentionality, which is the defining characteristic of consciousness.

---

[138] .S. E. Stumpf, p. 490.
[139] .Ibid, 491.

The *epoche* serves as a starting point as it provides and guarantees the kind of neutrality required by the phenomenological method because it is epistemologically impartial. It is, therefore, a necessary condition to all phenomenological procedures. The *epoche* leads us back to the center of reality, which is the conscious self. The *epoche* leads us into the method of reductions.

Husserl distinguishes three stages of reduction, which some writers usually collapse into two. They are:

i.   Phenomenal reduction
ii.   Eidetic reduction
iii. Transcendental reduction

Some writers collapse the phenomenal reduction into the natural attitude since the phenomenological procedure begins with the second stage and they talk about only two stages of reduction; the eidetic reduction and the transcendental reduction.

The Phenomenal Reduction

This is the stage through which we change all that is given in experience into a phenomenon. The phenomenon here is that which is known in and by consciousness, through intuition, recollection, and judgment.

The Eidetic Reduction

This is the second stage which consists in the movement from that which is given in experience to the essences of that which is given in experience. It is the movement from the empirical to the universal. The empirical is particular while the universal is essential. At this stage, the various acts of consciousness are made accessible in order that their essences can be grasped through the intuition of essences. The intuition of essences is the process by which we form a multiplicity of all the variations of that which is given while still maintaining this multiplicity of the given, we focus our attention on the residuum; that which remains unchanged in the multiplicity. The residuum is what Husserl calls the 'invariant'.

The Transcendental Reduction

The third stage, transcendental reduction, further reduces the residuum of the eidetic reduction to the transcendental ego through whose activity we grasp the world. At this stage, there is a phenomenological purification of the worldly subjectivity and temporality of the eidetic reduction. From this emerges the intentionality of consciousness. It is a movement from the perceptual immersion into the objects given in natural attitude to the reflective concern of consciousness itself. Therefore, it is no longer just a perceptual activity but 'my perceptual activity.' I am no longer just conscious but conscious of something, I am no longer just thinking, but thinking of something. This is the clearest fact of the human experience; the consciousness of something. This is what we referred to above as the *ergo cogito cogitatum* in distinction from the Cartesian *cogito ergo sum*. All the acts of consciousness are directed towards something. As Okeregbe puts it, "thus, all the activities of consciousness are conscious acts in relation to the ego, which *intends* them; all the process of *epoche* and reductions culminate in intentionality, which is the structure of consciousness."[140]

Intentionality

This is one of the central concepts of phenomenology. It is 'aboutness' or 'directedness' as exemplified by our mental states. Intentionality is the directedness towards a transcendental object. By intentionality, "Husserl means that any object of my consciousness, a house, a pleasure, a number, or another person, is something meant, constructed, constituted, that is, intended by me."[141] It is an intrinsic feature of intentional acts as against being in relation to the act. The clearest fact about our human experience is that consciousness is always consciousness of something; it is the essence of consciousness to point toward or intend some object. The very act of intending, which is the active involvement of the ego in creating our experience is what intentionality designates. According to Stumpf, Husserl sees intentionality as "the structure of consciousness itself and is also the

---

[140] .A. O. Okeregbe, p. 254.
[141] .S. E. Stumpf, p. 489.

fundamental category of being".[142] Therefore, intentionality is the way that subjects are in touch with the world.

The term intentionality was originally used by the Scholastics. It was revived by Brentano in the 19th Century. Husserl takes the concept from Brentano, although with some reservations. For instance, he maintains that most mental phenomena are intentional but not all. Pain and pleasure are mental phenomena but they are not intentional. He also agrees with Brentano that intentionality is a mark of something being mental. For Brentano, intentionality is a sufficient condition for an act to be mental, but it is not a necessary condition for an act to be mental. Husserl, however, disagrees with Brentano that every mental happening is a mental phenomenon.

Mental acts for Husserl are mental activities and not mental objects. Here Husserl makes a distinction between two senses of consciousness:

i. Consciousness as a permanent state of awareness
ii. Consciousness of one thing or another.

As (i), consciousness covers the entire stream of our experience, while as (ii), it is simply the inner perception of something, that is, the intentional relation to an object. Consciousness itself is "an inner experience made up of intentional acts and some experiences that are not intentional such as sensation, e.g. of pain, pleasure, happiness, sadness".[143] Consciousness has three aspects: (i) the subject of experience, (ii) the act of experience itself, and (iii) the object of experience. These correspond to the ego that experiences, the experience itself, and the intentional object to which the ego is directed.

The notion of intentionality draws our attention to the fact that all our beliefs, dreams, desires, and wishes, are about things and that even the words with which we express these beliefs and our mental states are about things. The usual problem that is associated with intentionality is the problem of comprehending the relationship between our mental states, or our expressions of our mental states, and the things our mental states are about. This relationship is

---

[142] .Ibid., p. 490
[143] .J. Omoregbe, ibid., p. 25

characterized by a number of peculiarities. For instance, if I have a relation with a chair by sitting on the chair, it means that the chair and I exist. But how do we characterize relations that have to do with fears, hopes, wishes, and even mental objects that have no concrete existence? Another peculiarity is that, for instance, given that the chair I sit on is the oldest antique in Nigeria, then, my relations with it would be that I am sitting on the oldest antique in Nigeria. How do we characterize when I plan to avoid a madman and the madman happens to be my friend; but I am not planning to avoid my friend, or can my plan to avoid the madman be interpreted as a plan to avoid my friend? According to Blackburn, the interpretation seems to depend on how the object is specified, or on the mode of presentation of the object.[144]

According to phenomenologists, intentionality is the characteristic of consciousness. This intentional character of consciousness is simply that consciousness or experience is an act of intention or intentional act with a purpose in the external world. Intentionality underlines the fact that no act of experience is in vain because it has a purpose, which is directed to something outside it. It is a logical fact that every experience must be an experience of something. It is the experience of something different and distinct from the act of experience itself. This implies that you cannot be conscious of nothing, every consciousness is consciousness about an object, and therefore, there is always an object of consciousness. For instance, to be conscious of a range rover car means the range rover car is the intentional object of one's thought. Same way, if one is conscious of a headache, the intentional object of one's consciousness is the head.

According to Owolabi, "the concept of intentionality therefore establishes that the activity of consciousness is not a lonely act but involves something outside it."[145] This means that consciousness as an intentional act is a projection towards something external to it. This indicates that there is a link between the act of consciousness and the external world. This link makes the act of consciousness an intentional correlation with the external world. Therefore,

---

[144] .S. Blackburn, p. 196.
[145] .K. Owolabi,[A] p. 283.

consciousness without the external world cannot be. We cannot have a thinker without a thought, and the thought is always about something, an object, different from the act of thinking, which is always outside the thought.

The essence of the notion of intentionality for phenomenology is that it first and foremost, establishes the fact that the object of consciousness is in logical correlation with the world. This enables the phenomenologists advance the argument that the subject of experience can, and does have a proper and adequate knowledge of phenomena or external objects, since they are intentional correlates. The implication of this for the Kantian noumenon-phenomenon distinction is that it makes the distinction a pseudo-problem. Intentionality, according to Owolabi, makes things as they are in themselves always reveal themselves to be properly experienced by their intentional correlates.

The second essence of the concept of intentionality is particularly relevant to the Husserlian epistemological project. The concept provides him the grounds to affirm the certainty of the subjective ego and the object of experience. This is because both the subjective ego and the object of experience are linked. Therefore, to accept one will necessarily mean to accept the other. This is why Husserl talks about *ergo cogito cogitatum* instead of the Cartesian *cogito ergo sum*. For Husserl, it is "I think of something" and not the Cartesian, "I think".

Apparently, the notion of intentionality is very germane to the phenomenology enterprise. It is embraced by all the strands of phenomenology; those with epistemic agenda like Husserl, or ontological, existential agenda, like Heidegger, Sartre and others. The latter category of phenomenologists sees the intentional relationship between the subjective ego and the external world as a support for the return of philosophy to confronting the issues that assail the individual. Sartre, for instance, asserts that intentionality plunges man back into the world as it gives full measure to man's agonies, sufferings, and also to his rebellion.[146]

---

[146] .J. P. Sartre (1957). *Transcendence of the Ego*, New York: Noonday Press, p. 105.

A Critical Review of Phenomenology

The phenomenological enterprise is an enticing one, but with an over blown ambition. Its fundamental objective to know phenomenon as it is by adopting a presuppositionless approach to objects of cognition sounds a great idea. The question, however, is whether this is possible. Can we really devoid ourselves of prior beliefs and ideas in relation to the objects of cognition? Can we ever be free of presumptions? Are presumptions not even cognitive aids in the sense that they set the stage for investigation and enquiry into given phenomena?

The fact is that presuppositions are necessary for interpretation and in most cases, if not all, we employ them unconsciously. I think it is overly ambitious to think that we can, as humans, devoid ourselves completely of our presuppositions. While I will concede to the fact that our correct apprehension of phenomena can be blurred by prior beliefs and suppositions, we also have to admit that they can also assist positively in understanding correctly the objects of cognition.

It is interesting to note that even phenomenology did not succeed in adopting the presuppositionless approach in fashioning its teaching. Let us take a closer look at Husserl's notion of *epoche*, for instance. It is a product of his mathematical mind. He carried it over to philosophy. He simply brought the idea of parenthesis in mathematics and adapted it in dealing with how we understand the essences of phenomena. He is guilty of employing prior suppositions and beliefs in the enquiry into objects of cognition.

We need to ask the important question, whether philosophy can adopt the scientific method of description without losing its own essence and autonomy. Philosophy is, by nature, rigorously speculative, it is in the essence of philosophy to be speculative and rationally critical. To seek to be descriptive is to seek to be like the natural and empirical sciences. This will definitely rob philosophy of its essential nature. The problems that philosophy investigates are mostly controversial and indeterminate and they can never be approached like the empirical sciences. We cannot make prescriptions in philosophy. Neither can we afford to run a closed system of thought. Philosophy must always be open to new ideas and possibilities as knowledge is inexhaustible and fresh waters can always come forth from its fountains.

The linguistic turn in philosophy pioneered by the advocates of the analysis of language as a proper method of doing philosophy in the likes of Wittgenstein, Russell, Moore, and others, have brought to the fore the necessity to employ clear use of language in expressing philosophical thought. We cannot but admit that phenomenology falls short of clear language of expression. The language of phenomenology is obscure and difficult. Thinkers in the phenomenological movement employ the use of a number of concepts from private vocabulary, like the term *epoche*, by Husserl, for instance. Many of these concepts are not clearly explained. This makes comprehending their thought difficult and almost impossible at times. Phenomenologists rely too much on technical language, and nonchalantly so, to the detriment of the movement.

These criticisms notwithstanding, we cannot deny the fact that phenomenology has contributed in some positive sense to the development of philosophy. The contribution of phenomenology would, however, be more appreciated if phenomenology has been couched in clearer language. While we are not canonizing linguistic analysis as 'the paradigm' of assessing proper philosophizing, we need to affirm the fact that philosophical language needs to be clear and lucid. Phenomenology failed in this direction.

PART THREE

HERMENEUTICS

Chapter

7

Philosophical Hermeneutics

Introduction

The term hermeneutics is broadly understood to mean the art of interpreting texts. It traditionally refers to the study of the interpretation of written texts, especially in the areas of literature, religion, and law.[147] Hermeneutics studies the theory and practice of interpretation. According to the *Internet Stanford Encyclopedia of Philosophy*, "it covers both the first order and second order theory of understanding and interpretation of linguistic and non-linguistic expressions."[148]

The practice of hermeneutics dates back to ancient Greek philosophy as a theory of interpretation. Its etymology is traced back to the Greek mythological god, Hermes, who was both the messenger amongst the gods, on the one hand, and between the deities and humans, on the other hand. It is this god that leads souls to the underworld after death and he is credited to have invented language and speech. He is reputed to be an interpreter, a liar, a thief, and a trickster.

In the middle ages and the Renaissance, hermeneutics turned out as an important branch of Biblical studies, which later included the study of ancient and classic cultures. With the German Romanticism

---

[147] ."Hermeneutics" in www.en.wikipedia.org/wiki/Hermeneutics (Retrieved on 11/4/13).
[148] "Hermeneutics" in www.plato.stanford.edu/entries/hermeneutics/(Retrieved on 11/4/13).

and idealism, its status changed; it became philosophical. It was now conceived as the conditions of possibility for symbolic communication and no longer just a methodological or didactic aid for other disciplines.

With the change in status, there was a change in the question of interest from "how to read" to "how we communicate at all." Therefore, in modern times, hermeneutics refers to everything within the interpretative process, be it verbal or non-verbal forms of communication and all aspects of communications, like presuppositions, preunderstandings, the meaning and philosophy of language, and semantics.[149]

The shift in the meaning of hermeneutics was occasioned by the likes of Friedrich Schleiermacher, Wilhelm Dilthey and others. This, in turn, triggered off the ontological turn that Martin Heidegger's *Being and Time* brought into the understanding of hermeneutics in the 1920s and later promoted by Hans-Georg Gadamer in his *Truth and Method*. Heidegger shifted the focus of philosophical hermeneutics from interpretation to existential understanding. Hermeneutics, for him, was a direct, non-mediated, that is, more authentic, way of being in the world, than simply a way of knowing.[150]

Thus, Heidegger went beyond symbolic communication to something more fundamental, namely, the issue of human existence. Hermeneutics, therefore, became a kind of interrogation into the deepest conditions for symbolic interaction and culture in general.[151] It is within this new context of understanding the term hermeneutics that the horizon for many of the most intriguing discussions of contemporary philosophy, which covered both the Anglo-American context (Rorty, McDowell, and Davidson) and Continental discourse (Habermas, Apel, Ricoeur and Derrida), is situated.

---

[149] . S. B. Ferguson, D. F. Wright, and J. I. Packer (1988). *New Dictionary of Theology*, Illinois: Intervarsity Press.
[150] M. Heidegger (1927). *Being and Time*, Harper and Row, p. H125.
[151] "Hermeneutics" in www.plato.stanford.edu/entries/hermeneutics/(Retrieved on 11/4/13).

The Concept and Development of Hermeneutics

Hermeneutics is the Latinized version of the Greek word, *hermeneuein*, which has been part of the everyday language since the 17th Century. It means to translate, or interpret, or make intelligible.[152] In line with this etymology, it is understood as an inquiry into the nature or methods of interpretation. Although as a practice, it predates the 17th Century because Plato used it in a number of his dialogues. The word 'hermeneutics,' itself, was first used by J. C. Dannhauer. According to Dannhauer, three kinds of texts require a theory of interpretation. They are (i) Holy Scripture, (ii) Legal texts, and (iii) literature of classical antiquity. While Plato never really used the word 'hermeneutics', he, however, reflected on the art of the interpretation of texts. He compared hermeneutical knowledge to *Sophia*. For Plato, hermeneutical knowledge was revealed and it was religious, while *Sophia* was knowledge of the truth-value of utterance. Aristotle moved it a step further when he titled his work on logic and semantics *Peri Hermeneias* which means *On Interpretation*. With the advent of the Stoics, hermeneutics gradually took on the idea of a methodological awareness of the problems of textual understanding, although they (Stoics) did not develop a systematic theory of interpretation; Philo of Alexandria did.

The two prominent names whose thoughts indicated reference to hermeneutics in medieval philosophy are Augustine and Aquinas. Augustine had a profound influence on the understanding of modern hermeneutics. He introduced the universality-claim of hermeneutics through the connection he established between language and interpretation and from his claim that the interpretation of scripture consists in a deeper, existential level of self-understanding. Aquinas also had an impact on the development of modern hermeneutics. He questioned the authenticity of certain pseudo-Aristotelian texts by comparing them to the existing Aristotelian corpus. By doing so, he anticipated a critical-philological procedure. This became a crucial aspect of Schleiermacher's notion of grammatical interpretation.

---

[152] .T. Mautner, "Hermeneutics", p. 248.

Traditional hermeneutics had two aims that were radically different. These aims correspond to the two main areas that traditional hermeneutics was concerned with; namely, theology and jurisprudence. One of the two aims of traditional hermeneutics was to provide a correct interpretation, and the other aim was to establish an authoritative statement of dogma or law.[153] It is difficult to satisfy these two aims or requirements. Hence, hermeneutics was considered, in the traditional context, as the art of finding something in a text that is not in the text.

The development of early modern hermeneutics is found in Martin Luther's *Sola Scriptura*. Based on his emphasis on faith and inwardness, the authority of the traditional interpretations of the Bible was questioned. Luther wanted to emphasize that each reader of the Bible had to face the challenge of making the truths of the Bible his own. The reader is not bound to understand the text on the basis of being faithful to the predominant or authorized readings of the time. For him, each reader must make out his or her own path to the potential meaning and truth of the text. This made reading a problem in a new way.[154]

Furthering this thought, Giambattisto Vico argued against the Cartesianism of his time. According to him, thinking is rooted in a given context and the given context is historically developed and intrinsically related to ordinary language as it has evolved from the myths and poetry of the people to the theoretical abstraction and modern vocabulary. This implies that to understand oneself is to understand the origin of one's own intellectual horizon. Therefore, self-understanding and understanding cannot be separated. "Self-understanding is oriented towards who we are, living, as we do, within a given historical context of practice and understanding."[155]

Along with Luther and Vico, Spinoza also contributed to the development of the early stages of modern hermeneutics. In his *Tractatus Theologico-Politicus* (1670), he argued, in chapter 7, that we have to keep in view the historical horizon in which the texts were

---

[153] Ibid.
[154] "Hermeneutics" in www.plato.stanford.edu/entries/hermeneutics/(Retrieved on 11/4/13).
[155] Ibid.

written and the mind of the authors in order to understand the most dense and difficult sections of scriptures. According to him, to understand the parts, we need to understand the whole, and the whole can only be understood on the basis of the parts. This is what is referred to as the *hermeneutic circle*. The hermeneutic circle is the movement between the parts and the whole of the text. It refers to the problems we encounter in the process of interpretation. This is the case, when for instance, in a text, we can only understand one element in terms of the meanings of other elements or the whole text. And we cannot even understand the other elements or the whole text without understanding the original element in question. This is an important theme in hermeneutics, which we shall discuss below.

It is worthy to note that Luther, Vico, and Spinoza shaped and gave direction to modern hermeneutics. They did not develop any explicit philosophical theory of understanding; neither did they outline a method or a set of normatively binding rules to guide the process of interpretation. Johann Martin Chladenius was the first to do this when he distinguished between hermeneutics and logic. According to him, variations in our perception of phenomena and problems bring about difficulties in our understanding of other people's texts and statements. He united hermeneutics and epistemology as he joined the search for truth and the search for understanding. This anticipated an important orientation in 20th Century hermeneutics, which is discussed below under the title, "Hermeneutics in Modern and Contemporary Times". Modern hermeneutics is built on the following pillars:

i.   The interest in the human sciences and willingness to defend the integrity of the human sciences as distinct from the natural sciences.
ii.   The deep concern with the problem of making sense of the texts handed over to us from the past.

The first attempt to articulate a genuinely philosophical hermeneutics starts at the point where these two orientations meet and mutually inform one another. And this was the period of the German romanticism and idealism. This is the subject of discussion in the section below.

Hermeneutics in Modern and Contemporary Times

In its historical evolution, hermeneutics has become associated and recognized as part of epistemology or a theory of knowledge. This is because it has come to be known as the study of the principles by which we obtain certain kinds of knowledge. Despite this understanding of hermeneutics, it is not universally agreed that interpretation provides knowledge. The lack of universal agreement that interpretation provides knowledge is a result of its incompatibility with three of the fundamental teachings of positivism, which enjoy wide acceptance. As such, positivists do not embrace this understanding of hermeneutics. The tenets of positivism that are at variance with the idea that interpretation provides some kind of knowledge are:

i.   That in principle, scientific method can and must be applied in all fields of inquiry in order to gain knowledge
ii. That the method of the physical sciences is the ideal paradigm
iii. That facts are to be explained causally, and that such an explanation consists in subsuming individual cases under general laws.[156]

Other than the conception of hermeneutics as a project in epistemology, it has also been understood as denoting an ontological inquiry. In this sense, hermeneutics is conceived as "a theory, which explores the kind of existence had by beings who are able to understand meanings, and to whom the world is primarily an object of understanding."[157] This notion avoids the question of perception, either as empiricism would refer to sense perception or rationalism would refer to mental constructs; instead, it talks of understanding, which is more in consonance with the existentialist agenda. Little wonder then, the likes of Heidegger are described as hermeneutical in this sense.

---

[156] . T. Mautner, "Hermeneutics", p. 248.
[157] Ibid., p. 249

There has been a distinction between the hermeneutics of tradition and hermeneutics of suspicion. This distinction is traced to Paul Ricoeur. According to him, the hermeneutics of tradition pays attention to what is communicated. It aims to listen intently to that which is communicated with the intention of gaining an insight from it or becoming aware of the message that is hidden under the surface. This strand or tendency of hermeneutics is represented by Gadamer, whose version of hermeneutics is discussed below. The other strand, the hermeneutics of suspicion seems subversive, in the sense that it attempts to show that texts and human action are not completely harmless, as they seem to be. But that they may in fact, be reflections of hidden drives and class interests, or even much more. This perspective of hermeneutics is represented by the likes of Nietzsche, Freud, and Foucault. There is another strand of hermeneutics referred to as critical hermeneutics represented by Habermas and Apel. This strand continues in the tradition of ideological criticism that is traceable to the 18th Century. Its aim is to criticize existing socio-political and cultural conditions through interpretations that demystify such sociopolitical conditions. Karl Marx practiced this kind of hermeneutics.

The three very prominent names in modern hermeneutics are Friedrich Schleiermacher, Wilhelm Dilthey, and Martin Heidegger. The outline of philosophical hermeneutics laid down by these thinkers is further developed in the works of more contemporary thinkers like Hans-Georg Gadamer and Jurgen Habermas.

Friedrich Schleiermacher (1768-1834)

Schleiermarcher was the first major thinker to propose a theory of textual interpretation. He transcended the traditional view by pulling together all the intellectual currents of the time so as to articulate a coherent conception of a universal hermeneutics. By universal hermeneutics, we mean a hermeneutics that does not relate to a particular kind of textual material like the Bible or any ancient text, but to linguistic meaning in general. In this project, Schleiermarcher argues that "interpretation requires not only a proper grasp of the relevant linguistic and historical facts, but also a mental retracing, an imaginative reconstruction, of the way in which a text came into being".[158] In his view, we cannot take the understanding of other cultures for granted. Therefore, the interpreter of a text needs to be in a position to see and understand the life of the author and his work as a whole, and be able to place both within a historical setting. This kind of knowledge, which is apparently not attainable to the author himself, places the interpreter in the vantage position to understand the text even better than the author.

According to him, therefore, we need an openness to understand others. This openness makes it possible for us to realize that what looks natural, true, or coherent may cover something deeply unfamiliar. The kind of openness we talk about here can be achieved, if we scrutinize our own hermeneutic prejudices. This would involve a strict practice of hermeneutics, which even still does not guarantee a just or fully adequate understanding; nonetheless, such a strict practice is an indispensable aid. It helps the hermeneutician to avoid the error of using his own cultural, theological, or philosophical frame of mind as a frame or filter of another's speech or writing.

According to Schleiermacher, any use of language is between the radical individuality and the radical universality. None of these two poles exists in an entirely purified form. The individuality of language-use is not a reference to an inner, inaccessible layer of the mind, but a reference to something like the style, the voice, or the particularity of the language as used or applied.

Based on the above, Schleiermacher argues that to get the meaning of another person's speech or text, we need to focus on the two aspects of the person's language-use. These two aspects are:

i.   The shared resources or grammar and syntax
ii.   The individual application.

For Schleiermacher, this is the task of combining grammatical and technical interpretation. And in his opinion, there is no rule for this combination. What happens is that we compare the text with other texts from the same period, from the same writer, while we keep constantly in sight the uniqueness of the particular work in question. He refers to this as the capacity for divination. By divination he

---

[158] .T. Mautner, "Hermeneutics", p. 248.

simply means the ability to move from particular to universal with the aid of general rules or doctrines. This movement or divination is done by a comparative approach combined with a creative hypothesis-making. It is only by this that we can get a better understanding. Better understanding here does not necessarily imply a fully adequate understanding. According to Schleiermarcher, when we misunderstand, we are not totally alienated or cut away from that which we misunderstand. We are ordinarily able to communicate most times, successfully, without fully understanding the issue of our discussion. To understand better does not necessarily imply that we have a fully adequate understanding. This, in itself, does not imply that understanding is never final or can never be fully adequate.

Wilhelm Dilthey (1833-1911)

After Schleiermacher, Dilthey and others further developed the concept of hermeneutics. The historian, J. G. Droysen, with particular reference to historical knowledge, stressed that the knowledge gained by interpretation is different from scientific knowledge. Dilthey developed this view further and firmly established it when he explained it as the contrast between understanding and explanation. While the knowledge gained from interpretation is denoted by understanding, scientific knowledge is denoted by explanation. According to Dilthey, knowledge of historical, social, and cultural facts is essentially knowledge gained through interpretation. And this, in his opinion, explains why such historico-social and cultural knowledge is radically different from the knowledge of the sciences, which is a product of the application of the scientific method.

He and his compatriots basically returned to Vico's old problem. This is the problem of how to philosophically justify and account for the particular kind of objectivity in relation to the study of man. While Vico was interested in culture and history at large, Dilthey and others were more specifically focused on "how to justify the humanities within a university system that is based upon the

Enlightenment ideals of critical reason and rationality, and no longer on authority, tradition, and theological canon?"[159]

Dilthey moved the search for philosophical legitimation of the human sciences further by arguing that the scientific explanation of nature must be completed with a theory of how the world is given to us through symbolically mediated practices. [160] This is what the philosophy of the humanities is aimed at; providing such a theory. With Dilthey, hermeneutics has become "a theory of interpretation of all bearers of meaning: not only texts but also human action and the various features of human culture and society."[161]

Martin Heidegger (1889-1976)

The arrival of Heidegger on the scene completely transformed the discipline of hermeneutics. Hermeneutics for Heidegger, "is not a matter of understanding linguistic communication, neither is it about providing a methodological basis for the human sciences ... hermeneutics is ontology; it is about the most fundamental conditions of man's being in the world." [162] Though we refer to Heidegger's position as a complete transformation, it was not completely severed from earlier hermeneutical philosophies.

Heidegger talks about the hermeneutics of facticity as that which philosophy is all about. He considered terms like understanding, interpretation, and assertion from new points of view and meaning. For him, understanding is a mode of being and not a method of reading or the outcome of a willed and carefully conducted procedure of critical reflection. Understanding is not something we do consciously or fail to do; understanding is something that we are. It is a characteristic of the being human being, of *Dasein*.

According to Heidegger, the world is familiar to us in a basic, intuitive way. It is tacitly intelligible to us. This implies that we do not understand the world through a collection of neutral facts, which in

---

[159] "Hermeneutics" in www.plato.stanford.edu/entries/hermeneutics/ (Retrieved on 11/4/13).
[160] . Ibid.
[161] .T. Mautner, "Hermeneutics", p. 248.
[162] "Hermeneutics" in www.plato.stanford.edu/entries/hermeneutics/ (Retrieved on 11/4/13).

turn helps us to reach a set of universal propositions, laws, or judgments that correspond to the world as it is. We are fundamentally familiar with the world and this familiarity with the world is brought to reflective consciousness through interpretation. This implies that interpretation makes things, objects, and the fabric of the world, appear as something.

The synthesizing activity of understanding discloses the world to us as a totality of meaning; a space in which *Dasein* is at home. Assertion brings the synthesizing activity of understanding and interpretation to language. Therefore, while interpretation discloses the meaning of a thing, assertion discloses the meaning through language or brings down the meaning linguistically. It means then that the linguistic identification of a thing is predicated on the world-disclosive synthesis of understanding and interpretation. This also applies to the truth-value of the assertion. This means that the world-disclosive truth of understanding is more fundamental than the truth as presented in the propositional structure "S is P".

In this way, Heidegger reformulates the problem of truth, which gives rise to a new way of understanding the hermeneutic circle. Prior to this, the hermeneutic circle was understood as the mutual relationship between the text and tradition. Now with Heidegger's reformulation, based on the ontological turn, the hermeneutic circle refers to "the interplay between our self-understanding and our understanding the world."[163] Therefore, the hermeneutic circle now entails an existential task that confronts each one of us.

Heidegger argues that the self-interpretatory endeavours of *Dasein* distinguish it. *Dasein* is fundamentally embedded in the world, therefore, we cannot understand ourselves without understanding the world and the world cannot be understood without reference to *Dasein*'s way of life. This is a perpetual process. What is precarious in this process is how to enter the hermeneutic circle in the right way and not when our interpretative endeavours will lead us to a clear, lucid, and indubitable understanding of the meaning of the text, and therefore, enable us to leave the hermeneutic circle. To enter the hermeneutic circle in the right way entails a willingness to realize, on our part, that the investigation into the ontological conditions of our

---

[163] .Ibid.

life ought to work back on the way our life is led. This is precisely the turn towards ontology, which makes the problem of philology secondary. Hermeneutics, within this context, now deals with the meaning or the lack of meaning of human life, for it has now taken on an existential task.[164]

Hans-Georg Gadamer (1900-2002)

He was a student of Heidegger who took over from where Heidegger left off. He worked within the paradigm of Heidegger, accepting fully the ontological turn in hermeneutics. At the same time, however, he wanted to investigate the consequences of this turn for our understanding of the human sciences. To successfully do this, he went back to Vico and the neo-Aristotelian strands of early modern humanism. Hence, his work was considered as 'hermeneutics humanism'. Gadamer tried to synthesize the Heideggerian notion of the world-disclosive synthesis of understanding with the idea of *Bildung*, of education in culture. He spent more than thirty years working on and completing this project, which is articulated in his *Wahrheit und Methode – Truth and Method* (1960).

According to Gadamer, the human being is a being in language. Language opens up the world for us. We learn to master the world by learning to master a language. We can only really understand ourselves when we understand ourselves as beings situated within a linguistically mediated historical culture. Language is, therefore, our second nature.

The implication of this for our understanding of the human sciences, namely, art, culture, and historical texts, is that, ever before we get the chance to approach these human sciences objectively, they have already shaped our world-view. This is because, as part of our tradition, historical works, apart from presenting themselves to us as neutral and value-free objects of scientific investigation, also constitute part of the horizon in which we live, and therefore, shape our world-view.

Gadamer opines that we never know a historical work as it originally appeared to its contemporaries. This is so because we lack

---

[164] Ibid.

access to its original context of production or to the intentions of its author. Tradition is not passive or stifling; it is always alive, productive and in constant development. It is, therefore, a waste of effort to try to locate the scientific value of the humanities in their capacity for objective reconstruction as the earlier Hermeneuticians did. We get to know the past through the ever-changing and complex fabric of interpretations; this gets richer and even more complex as the decades and centuries roll by. History is always effective and never deficient; it is a unique possibility that involves the truth of self-understanding.

The point that Gadamer is making is that, we are conditioned by our position in history in such a way that we cannot return to the perspective of past authors. Nonetheless, we can still understand their works because our conditioning actually facilitates the understanding as it opens the world to us. We can truly understand the meaning of a text or event if we relate it to our own concepts, preconceptions, and prejudices. Therefore, the interpreter spells out the meaning of a text in his own historical situation.

As far as Gadamer is concerned, rather than the human person addressing the text of tradition, the texts of tradition actually address the human person. The texts of tradition address us because they have passed through decades and centuries. Precisely because of this, the texts of tradition, that is, classic works of art, literature, science, and philosophy, question our 'us' and our way of life. These texts expose our prejudices and the aspects of our cultural horizon that we take for granted. Historical texts have an authority that precedes our own; this authority is kept alive only to the extent that we recognize it in the present.

How do we recognize this authority? We do by engaging with the text in a textual explication and interpretation; that is, by entering into a relationship of dialogue with the past. This is what Gadamer calls "the fusion of horizons." It is a movement of understanding through interpretation between the present and the past. As we come through interpretation to understanding, what seems initially alien becomes richer and encompassing in meaning. We then begin to gain a better and more profound understanding of the text and also of ourselves. In the fusion of the horizons what appeared initially distant and alien emerges as a function of the limitations of our own initial point of departure.[165]

We successfully obtain the fusion of horizons when we engage with the text in a productive way. We do this through tacitly following the example of others and not through mastering a certain doctrine, method, or theory; it involves a practical know-how like the Aristotelian *phronesis*. It is a kind of knowledge that cannot be theoretically deduced or be fully articulated. It depends on tact and sensitivity that is only exhibited in the form of exemplary judgments and interpretations.[166]

Therefore, Gadamer evolves his own version of the hermeneutic circle, that is, the co-determination of text and reader. For Gadamer, the way our reading contributes to the affective history by adding to the complexity and depth of the meaning of the text is as important as the interplay between the parts and the whole of a text. We cannot grasp the meaning of a text once and for all, because the meaning of a text exists in the complex dialogical interplay between the past and the present. For Gadamer, therefore, we can never necessarily and constitutively obtain a conclusive self-knowledge just as we can never master the text of the past. Knowledge of tradition and knowledge of ourselves are interminable processes; tasks without determinate end-points. This is Gadamer's humanistic ontology, that our being is historically conditioned to be always more being than conscious being.

Jurgen Habermas (1929-   )

Habermas and Karl-Otto Apel represent the Frankfurt school, which criticized the humanistic ontological turn brought into the understanding of hermeneutics by Gadamer. Habermas refers to Gadamer's hermeneutics as politically naïve. In his opinion, Gadamer does not give room for critical judgment and reflection in his hermeneutics because he placed too much emphasis on the authority of tradition. This denies reason the power of a critical and distanced judgment. According to Habermas, we need a set of quasi-transcendental principles of validity with which we can evaluate the

---

[165] .Ibid.
[166] .Ibid.

claims of tradition, and not just an analysis of the way history conditions us. Habermas argues that we need a critical theory of society to complete hermeneutics.

Note that Habermas does not completely dismiss Gadamer's approach to hermeneutics as mistaken. Rather, his argument is that Gadamer ascribes an illegitimate universality to hermeneutics. To solve this, Habermas argues that we require an adequate standard of validity, which he calls the quasi-transcendental principles of communicative reason. This will help the social sciences guide hermeneutics to adequately serve the purpose of emancipation and social liberation. Note the socio-political undertone of Habermas argument. This confirms that he, Habermas, represents the strand of hermeneutics identified above as critical hermeneutics that engages in ideological criticisms.

In response to Habermas' criticism, Gadamer emphasizes that he does not advocate that we dispense with validity, objectivity, and method in understanding. According to him, anyone who interprets his position as such has simply misread him. Clarifying his position further, Gadamer reiterates that our situatedness within history is not a limiting condition only. As well as limiting us, it also opens up the world to us, in the sense that, it is the space within which, we have our human experience and reason.

Conclusion

Existentialism, Phenomenology, and Hermeneutics: A Synthesis

Richard Bernstein rightly observes that a central claim in Gadamer's philosophical hermeneutics is that understanding, interpretation, and application go together. This is against the older traditional claim that divides hermeneutics into understanding, interpretation, and application, as three distinct and independent activities. Gadamer argues that they are not independent and as such should not be considered or relegated to different sub-disciplines; they are internally related.[167]

Understanding of the condition of the human person in the world, which existentialists refer to as 'existence', is the central concern of existentialism. As a movement in philosophy, existentialism directs our attention to the fact of our existence and makes postulations on how to confront the various issues and problems related to us in order to fulfil our being. In this process, many of the existentialists adopt the phenomenological method.

The phenomenological method, which is articulated in the works of Husserl, is about evolving an appropriate method by which we can arrive at the essence of phenomena. The ultimate goal is to arrive at the knowledge of things as they are in themselves, which earlier thoughts, like that of Kant, for instance, have dismissed as impossible.

It is not strange to see some names of great thinkers cutting through these three lines of thought we have discussed above in their philosophizing. Prominent among these thinkers is Heidegger, who triples as an existentialist, a phenomenologist, and a hermeneutician.

---

[167] R. J. Bernstein (1986). *Philosophical Profiles: Essays in a Pragmatic Mode*, Cambridge: Polity Press, p. 94.

This is possible because there is an interconnection between these movements and thoughts. Bernstein's submission above, in a subtle manner, points to this interconnection. It is all about understanding, interpretation, and application.

Robert Solomon writes that "twentieth century existentialism has been greatly influenced by the method known as phenomenology, originated by Edmund Husserl and pursued into the existential realm by his student Martin Heidegger."[168] The phenomenological method of Husserl is about finding and examining the essential structure of experience. This is aimed at establishing universal truths that are necessary for basic consciousness. Heidegger tapped into this method and applied it to questions about the nature of human life. These questions range from the meaning of life to the nature and implication of death.

Heidegger replaces the Cartesian idea of the *cogito ergo sum* (I think, therefore, I am) with the concept of *Dasein*; his notion of man as a being-in-the-world. This implies rejection of a consciousness that is separate from the world in which we find ourselves 'abandoned.' So, Heidegger set out to deal with the ontological problem of *Dasein*, which is to find out who we are, and what we are to do with ourselves. Nietzsche refers to this as 'how to become what we are.' Therefore, phenomenology was for Heidegger, a method which helps us in disclosing our being. This is what he referred to as the world-disclosive.

Sartre also adopted the phenomenological method in expounding his existentialist notion. Using the phenomenological method, he defends his central thesis that human beings are essentially free. He 126*An Introduction to Existentialism, Phenomenology, and Hermeneutics* did not quite agree with Heidegger's rejection of the Cartesian *cogito* in relation to consciousness, rather he argues that "consciousness is such (as 'being-for-itself') that it is always free to choose (though not free not to choose) and free to 'negate' the given features of the world."[169] What Sartre implies here is that, whether we are cowardly or shy, or we are courageous and bold is a matter of how we choose to behave and that we can always also choose to change such

---

[168] .R. Solomon (2000). "Existentialism" in T. Mautner, ibid., p. 187.
[169] .Ibid., p. 188.

behaviour. As to situations that we cannot change, like, whether we are born Nigerians or Ghanaians, white or coloured, crippled or blind; the question is always open as to what we make of such situation. There are always alternatives as to whether we resign to the situation or make the best out of it positively. Between these alternatives, there is always room to make a choice.

The application of the phenomenological method by these existentialists found its way into the philosophical hermeneutics of Gadamer, who took after his teacher, Heidegger. Following the Heideggerian paradigm, which introduced the ontological turn into hermeneutics, Gadamer evolved what is later referred to as the 'hermeneutic humanism.' He explores the consequences of the ontological turn in hermeneutics for our understanding of the human sciences. On this, he elaborates the Heideggerian idea that all knowing and doing involves understanding and interpretation.

Gadamer, therefore, develops the idea that the theory of understanding and interpretation (hermeneutics) is not just about procedures and methods governed by rules, to ensure the objectivity of the human sciences, as opposed to the natural sciences. Rather, it is about fundamental skills that are manifest in the actions of human beings, who are self-conscious, linguistic animals. For Gadamer, these skills and the exercise of the skills give the essential historical character to human existence.

Although Donald Davison, who belongs to the analytic tradition, differs from Gadamer in terms of theoretical interest, Davidson, nonetheless, agrees with Gadamer that we understand others basically by drawing a relationship between their words and the world around them. Davidson refers to this as 'Radical Interpretation.' For him, "the contents of our thoughts, and so of our very recognition of the words of others and events to which they refer, themselves depend on our sharing with others a pattern of interaction with the world."[170]This, for Davidson, is triangulation.

It is clear that there is a nexus between existentialism, phenomenology, and hermeneutics. The trio are apparently concerned with the human being in his or her existential self, in

---

[170]   "Hermeneutics"   in   www.plato.stanford.edu/entries/hermeneutics (Retrieved on 11/12/13).

relation to others, and to the world. A proper understanding of self, others, and the world, would, no doubt, facilitate a more conducive and humane environment and this will better the lot of the human person. While efforts in these three philosophical discourses have not gone without criticisms, the endeavours of thinkers in these areas are definitely not futile. Criticisms are essentially part of the enterprise of philosophy and they serve the important purpose of leaving the issue of discourse open for further discussion.

Bibliography

Agidigbi, B. 2006. *Issues and Themes in Existentialist Philosophy*. Benin City: Skylight Prints.

Appignanesi, R. 2006. *What Existentialists Believe?* London: Granta Publications.

Aron, R. 1968. *Marxism and the Existentialists*. New York: Harper and Row.

Barnes, H. 1967. *An Existentialist Ethics*. New York: Knopf.

Barret, W. 1962. *Philosophy in the 20th Century*. Vol.3, New York: Random House. Beauvoir, S. D. 1948. *The Ethics of Ambiguity*. Citadel.

Bernstein, R. J. 1983. *Beyond Objectivism and Relativism*. Philadelphia: University of Pennsylvania Press.

_____. 1986. *Philosophical Profiles: Essays in a Pragmatic Mode*. Cambridge: Polity Press.

Blackburn, S. 1996. *Oxford Dictionary of Philosophy*. Oxford: Oxford University Press.

Bruns, G. 1992. *Hermeneutics: Ancient and Modern*. New Haven: Yale University Press.

Buber, M. 1978. *Between Man and Man*. Trans. by Ronald Gregor Smith. New York: Macmillan.

_____. 1970. *I and Thou*. Trans. Walter Kaufmann. New York: Scribner.

Camus, A. 1955. *The Myth of Sisyphus and Other Essays*. Trans. Justin O' Brien. New York: Knopf.

_____. 1988. *The Stranger*. Trans. Matthew Ward. New York: Knopf.

Cooper, D. E. 1999. *Existentialism*. Oxford: Blackwell.

Crowell, S. 2001. *Husserl, Heidegger, and the Scope of Meaning: Paths Toward Transcendental Phenomenology*. Evanston: Northwestern

University Press. Davidson, D. 2001. *Inquiries into Truth and Interpretation*. 2nd ed. Oxford: Clarendon Press.

Desan, W. 1954. *The Tragic Final*. Cambridge: University Press.

Dilthey, W. 1996. *Hermeneutics and the Study of History*. Eds. Rudolf A. Makkreel and Frithjof Rodi. New Jersey: Princeton University Press.

_____. 1989. *Introduction to the Human Sciences*. Eds. Rudolf A. Makkreel and Frithjof Rodi. New Jersey: Princeton University Press.

_____. 2002. *The Formation of the Historical World in the Human Sciences*. Eds. Rudolf A. Makkreel and Frithjof Rodi. New Jersey: Princeton University Press.

Donceel, J. F. 1967. *Philosophical Anthropology*. New York: Kansas.

Dostal, R. J. (Ed.) 2002. *The Cambridge Companion to Gadamer*. Cambridge: Cambridge University Press.

Earnshaw, S. 2006. *Existentialism: A Guide for the Perplexed*. London: Continuum. Edie, J. M. 1962. "Introduction" in Pierre Thevenaz. *What is Phenomenology? and Other Essays*. Ed. J. M. Edie, Chicago: Quadrangle Books.

Fell, J. 1979. *Heidegger and Sartre: An Essay on Being and Place*. New York: Columbia University Press.

Ferguson, S. B., Wright, D. F., and Packer, J. I. 1988. *New Dictionary of Theology*. Illinois: Intervarsity Press.

Flynn, T. 2006. *Existentialism: A Very Short Introduction*. Oxford: Oxford University Press.

Fuller, B. A. G. 1966. *A History of Philosophy*. 3rd Ed. New York: Holt, Rinehart and Winston.

Gadamer, H.-G. 1994. *Truth and Method*. Trans. by Joel Weinsheimer and Donald G. Marshall. New York: Continuum.

_____. 1986. *The Relevance of the Beautiful and Other Essays*. Ed. Robert Bernasconi. Trans. by Nicholas Walker. Cambridge: Cambridge University Press.

_____. 1976. *Philosophical Hermeneutics*. Trans. David E. Linge. Berkeley: University of California Press.

Gelven, M. 1990. *Truth and Existence: A Philosophical Inquiry*. University Park: Penn State Press.

Gordon, H. 1999. *Dictionary of Existentialism*. New York: Greenwood Press.

Grondin, J. 1995. *Sources of Hermeneutics*. New York: University of New York Press.

_____. 1994. *Introduction to Philosophical Hermeneutics*. New Haven: Yale University Press.

Guignon, C. 2003. *The Existentialists: Critical Essays on Kierkegaard, Nietzsch, Heidegger, and Sartre*. New York: Rowman and Littlefield.

Habermas, J. 1988. *On the Logic of the Social Sciences*. Trans. Shierry Weber Nicholsen and Jerry A. Stark. Cambridge: Polity Press.

Hahn, L. E. (ed.) 1997. *The Philosophy of Hans-Georg Gadamer: The Library of Living Philolsophers*. Vol. XXIV. Chicago: Open Court.

Hannay, A. 1982. *Kierkegaard*. London: Routledge.

Heidegger, M. 1962. *Being and Time*. Trans. John Macquarrie and Edward Robinson. San Fransico: Harper.

Hirsch, E. D. 1967. *Validity in Interpretation*. New Haven: Yale University Press.

Hollinger, R. (ed.). 1985. *Hermeneutics and Praxis*. Notre Dame: University of Notre Dame Press.

Husserl, E. 1970. *The Idea of Phenomenology*. Trans. William Alston and George Naknikian. The Hague: Martinus Nijhoff.

_____. 1969. *Ideas: General Introduction to Pure Phenomenology*. Trans. by W.R.Boyce Gibson. London: Allen and Unwin Ltd.

Jaspers, K. 1968. *Reason and Existenz*. New York: Noonday Press.

Kaufmann, W. 1968. *Existentialism from Dostoevsky to Sartre*. Cleveland: Meridian Books.

Kierkegaard, S. 1971. *Concluding Unscientific Postscript*. Trans. David F. Swenson and Walter Lowrie. Princeton: Princeton University Press.

_____. 1983. *Fear and Trembling*. Trans. by Howard V. Hong and Edna H.

Hong. Princeton: Princeton University Press.

_____. 1974. *Either/Or*. Vol. 2. Princeton: Princeton University Press.

Kisiel, T. 1993. *The Genesis of Heidegger's Being and Time*. Berkeley: University of California Press.

Kostenbaun, P. "Introductory Essay" in *The Paris Lectures*.

Makkreel, R. A. 1975. *Dilthey: Philosopher of the Human Sciences*. Princeton: Princeton University Press.

MacIntyre, A. 1967. "Existentialism" in *The Encyclopedia of Philosophy*. Vol. 3.

Ed. Paul Edwards. New York: Macmillan Publishing Co.

Macquarrie, J. 1983. *Existentialism*, New York: World Publishing Company. Marcel, G. 1968. *The Philosophy of Existentialism*. New York: Citadel Press.

Mautner, T. (ed.). 2000. *The Penguin Dictionary of Philosophy*. London: Penguin Books.

McBride, W. (ed.) 1997. *The Development and Meaning of Twentieth Century Existentialism*. New York: Garland Publishers.

Merleau-Ponty, M. 1962. *Phenomenology of Perception*. Trans. by Colin Smith. New York: Routledge and Kegan Paul.

Natason, M. 1968. *Literature, Philosophy, and the Social Sciences*. The Hague:

Martinus Nijhoff.

Nietzsche, F. 1969. *On the Geneology of Morals*. Trans. by Walter Kaufmann. New York: Vintage Books.

Nwachukwu, A. 1994. "Existentialist Themes in African Novel" in *Ufahamu: Journal of African Activist Association*. Vol. xiv, No. 1.

Nyong, D. 1996. *Rudiments of Philosophy and Logic*, Lagos: Obaroh and Ogbinaka Publishers Limited.

Okeregbe, A. O. 1996. "Phenomenology as Metaphysics" in J. I. Unah (ed.). *Metaphysics, Phenomenology and African Philosophy*, Ibadan: Hope Publications.

Olajide, W. 2000. "Existentialism" in K. A. Owolabi (ed.), *Issues and Problems in Philosophy*. Ibadan: GROVACS (NETWORK).

Omoregbe, J. I. 1991. *A Simplified History of Western Philosophy: Contemporary Philosophy*. Vol. 3. Lagos: Joja Educational Research and Publishers.

_____. 2001. *Philosophy of Mind: An Introduction to Philosophical Psychology*. Lagos: Joja Educational Research and Publishers Ltd.

Ormiston, G. L. and Alan, D. S. (eds.) 1990. *The Hermeneutic Tradition: From Ast to Ricoeur*. New York: State University of New York Press.

Owolabi, K. A. 1998. "The Phenomenological Movement" in A. Fadahunsi, (ed.), *Philosophy: An Anthology*. Lagos: ARK Publishers.

_____. 1992. "The Dichotomy between the Natural Attitude and

Phenomenological Attitude in the Philosophy of Edmund Husserl" in *The Nigerian Journal of Philosophy*. Vol.12, Nos.1 & 2. University of Lagos: Department of Philosophy.

Oyeshile, O. 2006. "An Existentialist Critique of Husserlian Phenomenological Approach to Knowledge" in R. A. Akanmidu (ed.). *Footprints in Philosophy*. Ibadan: Hope Publications.

Pence, G. 2000. *A Dictionary of Common Philosophical Terms*. New York: McGrawHill Companies Ltd.

Reynolds, J. 2006. *Understanding Existentialism*. London: Acumen.

Ricoeur, P. 1992. *Oneself as Another*. Trans. Kathleen Blamey. Chicago: University of Chicago Press.

Roberts, J. M. 1977. *Europe 1880 – 1945*. London: Longman.

Ronbczek, P. 1964. *Existentialism: For and Against*. Cambridge: University Press.

Rorty, R. 1991. *Essays on Heidegger and Others*. Cambridge: Cambridge University Press.

Sartre, J.-P. 1992. *Being and Nothingness*. Trans. by Hazel Barnes. New York:

Washington Square Press.

132   *An Introduction to Existentialism, Phenomenology, and Hermeneutics*
_____. 2007. *Existentialism is a Humanism*. Trans. Carol Macomber. New Haven: Yale University Press.

_____. 1968. *Search for a Method*, trans. by Harzel E. Barnes, New York: Vintage Books.

Schleiermarcher, F. 1998. *Hermeneutics and Criticism*. Ed. and Trans. by Andrew Bowie. Cambridge: Cambridge University Press.

_____. 1977. *Hermeneutics: The Handwritten Manuscripts*. Ed. by Heinz Kimmerle. Trans. by James Duke and Jack Forstman. Montana: Scholars Press.

Solomon, R. (ed.). 1974. *Existentialism*. New York: Random House.

Spiegelberg, H. 1984. *The Phenomenological Method*. 3rd Ed. The Hague: Martinus Nijhoff.

Stewart, D. and Mickunas, A. 1974. *Exploring Phenomenology: A Guide to the Field and Its Literature*. USA: American Library Association.

Stokes, P. 2012. *Philosophy: 100 Essential Thinkers*. London: Arcturus Publishing Ltd.

Stumpf, S. E. 1989. *Philosophy: History and Problems*, 4th Ed. New York: McGraw Hill Inc.

Tugendhat, E. 1992. "Heidegger's Idea of Truth." Trans. by Christopher Macann in Macann, Christopher (ed.). *Martin Heidegger: Critical Assessments*. 4 vols. London: Routledge.

Unah, J. I. 1996. "Phenomenology" in J. I. Unah, (ed.), *Metaphysics, Phenomenology and African Philosophy*. Ibadan: Hope Publications.

Vico, G. 1984. *The New Science of Giabattista Vico*. Trans. by Thomas Goddard Bergin and Max Harold Fisch. Ithaca: Cornell University Press.

Wachterhauser, B. R. (ed.). 1994. *Hermeneutics and Truth*. Evanston: Northwestern University Press.

_____. (ed.) 1986. *Hermeneutics and Modern Philosophy*. New York: State University of New York Press.

Wahl, J. 1949. *A Short History of Existentialism*. Trans. by Forrest Williams and Stanley Maron. New York: Philosophical Library.

Warnke, G. 1987. *Gadamer: Hermeneutics, Tradition, and Reason* Stanford: Stanford University Press.

Weate, J. (ed.). 1998. *A Young Person's Guide to Philosophy*, London: Dorling Kindersley.

Weinsheimer, J. C. 1985. *Gadamer's Hermeneutics*. New Haven. Yale University Press.

Wild, J. 1963. *The Challenge of Existentialism*. Bloomington: Indiana University Press.

Zaner, R. and Ihde, D. (eds.) 1973. *Phenomenology and Existentialism*. New York: Capricorn Books.

Internet Sources

"Atheistic Existentialism" in www.wikipedia.org

"Existentialism" in www.iep.utm.edu/existent/

"Existentialism" in www.thefreedictionary.com/existentialism

"Existentialism" in www.wikipedia.org

"Hermeneutics" in www.en.wikipedia.org/wiki/Hermeneutics

"Hermeneutics" in www.plato.stanford.edu/entries/hermeneutics/

"Phenomenology" in www.iep.utm.edu/phenom/

Smith, D. W. "Phenomenology", *The Stanford Encyclopedia of Philosophy* (Fall 2011 Edition), Edward N. Zalta (ed.), URL=<http://plato.stanford.edu/achives/fall2011/entries/phenomenology/>

Index